ETHICS

The Quest for the Good Life

ETHICS

The Quest for the Good Life

ETHICS

The Quest for the Good Life

by

Samuel L. Hart
Professor of Philosophy and Chairman,
Department of Philosophy,
Fairleigh Dickinson University

PHILOSOPHICAL LIBRARY
New York

Copyright, 1963, by
PHILOSOPHICAL LIBRARY, INC.
15 East 40th Street, New York 16, N.Y.

All rights reserved

170
H326 e

Library of Congress Catalog Card Number: 63-13347

Printed in the United States of America

To my Wife

TABLE OF CONTENTS

Introduction		1
Chapter		
I	Human Nature and Nurture	13
II	Moral Conduct	25
III	The Place of Emotions in Conduct	36
IV	The Place of Reason in Conduct	42
V	Freedom and License	48
VI	On Happiness	57
VII	Facts and Values	62
VIII	Good and Bad — Right and Wrong	74
IX	Ethical Relativism and Objective Ethics	81
X	Science and Ethics	94
XI	Ethics and Religion	107
XII	On Moral Progress — Toward a Universal Ethos	112
Notes		119
Index		125

INTRODUCTION

Our knowledge of nature increases daily. This continual progress is no mystery. We advance in natural sciences because we employ proper methods—those of experience and reason. Experience gives us facts, reason interprets them; experience discloses conjunctions, reason integrates them; experience points out similarities, reason helps us to keep them apart. Experience without reason is chaotic, reason without experience is empty. In natural sciences we have stopped being credulous. Facing perplexities, we do not conjure up our remote ancestors to answer our current problems. We look upon tradition as a vast repository of wisdom to be enriched by our own resourcefulness and inventiveness, and not as an ultimate legacy.

Our knowledge of man does not compare favorably with our knowledge of nature. The reasons for this undeniable fact are manifold. Man, no doubt, is a difficult subject to study. We cannot experiment with man as we do with natural phenomena. In human behavior multiple causation is the prevailing pattern, which of necessity gives our predictions a lower degree of probability. Our generalizations are bound to be more contingent. These are valid reasons for the slow advance of the science of man. But, as a rule, they handicap our progress less than artificially created and perpetuated obstacles. Admitting that man is a difficult subject to study, we must wonder at the innumerable voluminous treatises on man. Were such printed literary abundance an indication of the growth of reliable knowledge, we would have reason to rejoice. Unfortunately, this is not the case. Reliable knowledge is verified knowledge upon which we can act successfully. The prolific studies of man are not reliable. Hypotheses are heaped upon hypotheses without any attempt at verification. They are not projected as tentative solutions but rather as dogmatic assumptions or presumptions, as preconceived ideologies which reveal more the mentality of their creator than the structure and interconnection of social data.

The prevailing doctrines of man are not theories but forms of ideology. A scientific theory consists of ascertained facts, predictive confirmed generalizations, and hypotheses as tentative solutions of a conjectural nature. Scientific generalizations are never final. They are subject to correction and reinterpretation in accordance with new findings. Although there are many ways of discovering truth—from patient observation to occasional, genial insights—the methods and procedures of verification are the same. What renders a statement true is its correspondence with facts, its coherence with other true statements, and its pragmatic significance —that is, its ability to lead to successful action based on anticipated consequences.

The widespread bifurcation between ideologies of man and the theory of nature rests on the artificial dichotomy between facts and values. Values, we are told, cannot be scientifically investigated. They are subjective phenomena of emotive character, or socially conditioned responses. For lack of a theory of values which could guide man toward greater harmony and cooperation, social and political decisions are left to demagogues who accept that most damaging ideology, set forth by the Greek Sophists and by Machiavelli, that might makes anything right.

The divorce of politics from morality has devastating results: competition in evil doing, lack of mutual understanding, callousness to human misery, and endless bloody battles. Political Machiavellism finds support in hasty generalizations concerning heredity and environment, ethnic and racial groups, human motives and conflicts. Crimes and wars are ascribed to an innate pugnacity of man, to an unalterable destructiveness, although empirical findings indicate that gregariousness, cooperation, and aggression are conditioned patterns of behavior.

We hear a great deal about various cultures with diverse systems of values which are not susceptible of a trans-cultural appraisal. This has led to that false pride in scientific value-aloofness which is mainly responsible for the accumulation of social data devoid of any heuristic principle that could lead to a better understanding of these facts. This current scientific value-aloofness encourages people to whom we entrust our major conflicts in their amoral or immoral expediencies. They disregard warranted facts related to man's social behavior or misuse reason to justify their doings. Of what nature are these misuses of reason? All forms of rationalization. While reason clarifies our perplexities, rationalization keeps us confined to them. While reason is the major factor behind our intellectually cumulative experiences, rationalization undoes any value of learning. Reason is a healthy completion of experience, rationalization makes us retreat from reality. Reasoning converges toward truth, rationalization feeds on falsehood. As in the life of a single individual, so in the life of a social group or nation, rationalization is the poorest means of adjustment. We do not solve vital issues by circumventing or ignoring or disguising them.

Conflict is a concomitant feature of living. To try to eliminate it completely is to indulge in utopian dreams. But man has the power to mitigate conflicts, to reconcile opposing interests, to use his ingenuity and resourcefulness to make this planet a better place to live on. There need not be a gnawing despair or a fatalistic resignation if we learn to replace social or political shrewdness by intelligent behavior. The tremendous success natural science can justly take pride in, did not come as a gift from the blue sky. It has been the result of converging efforts of thousands of people, driven by the noble desire to alleviate man's struggle for survival. If we aspire to solve the many tragic social and political issues which beset mankind, we must adopt the same methods. We need a better founded knowledge of man, and men who are willing and able to apply such knowledge. Most of all, we need intellectual and moral integrity.

At a time when there was no science in the sense of a warranted body of knowledge arrived at by the methods of observation, experimentation, and valid reasoning, the subject matter of philosophy was unlimited. There was no physics but philosophies of nature; no psychology but philosophies of the mind; no social science but philosophies of human relations. Today we frown upon thinkers who indulge in free speculations about matter, its structure and transformations, about psychic functions and their interrelations, or about social accord and discord. But such past philosophical speculations turned out to be invaluable intellectual adventures, from which science developed. Although the results of these cognitive explorations are meager as compared to those of modern science, the high esteem in which we hold these predecessors of science is well deserved. They have engendered and kept alive the vital interest in knowing, in inquiring, and in examining.

Today the need for philosophical visions is not less urgent. But not in the fields of study where observation and experimentation are the most promising procedures to secure true and valid generalizations. Philosophical reflections are most needed in political, social, and moral issues, which, lacking exact, definite answers, require more scrutinized, bolder imaginative solutions. Without heuristic, guiding principles social data remain an amorphous mass devoid of any significance. What we need is a theory or theories of values that could assist us in framing social and political ideas capable of directing us toward a better individual and social integration. Pseudo-knowledge or faulty reasoning in decision making policies that affect our own life or the lives of millions lead to greater calamities than mistakes or miscalculations in physics. Such being the case, we cannot help wondering why man is most gullible and credulous where he can least afford to be—namely in his endeavor to secure and promote the good things in life. By his neglect or abandonment of the methods of rational, unbiased thinking, his goals and his aspirations are obscured or misguided.

Ethics or moral philosophy no matter how diversified the forms it has taken, no matter what its approaches have been to man's quest for the good life, has kept alive, in the past and in the present, the vital habit of critical thought concerning the perplexities of social existence. This is the most enduring legacy of the great ethical tradition, from Plato to Dewey. It was epitomized in the Socratic assertion that an unexamined life is not worth living. If we look for definite solutions, for final answers to the vexing problem of good and evil, right and wrong, for ultimate principles of conduct which could spare us the patient, untiring search for the moral requiredness of a given situation, the various ethical systems will disappoint us. Definite solutions are the proper domain of science. But even here ultimacy is a task rather than an achievement. The factually warranted beliefs of today become dubious tomorrow. Such is the career of truth itself, always evolving and expanding, always reaching its goal by approximation. A fact not to repine over. An ultimate truth would cut the life nerve of science.

Ethics is in no position to help us to reduce our moral decision-making to a mere logical game of subsuming particular instances under a general norm, for conditions and situations are unique, and moral principles can only serve as guideposts in the quest for fitting and unfitting behavior. There are no substitutes for moral reflection. Ethicists by upholding the rational ideal of responsible deliberation based on a broad imaginative survey of the possible consequences, help us to distinguish between opinions blurred by momentary impulses and wishes, and rational judgments, between mere guesses and tentative solutions, the success of which is predicated on the factual evidence.

Contemporary books on the good life are legion. Most of them are of an exhortatory nature. They espouse the good life in glittering generalities without any attempt at empirical evidence and logical clarity. Unfortunately, books aiming at ascertained knowledge and precision of language are written on a very high level of abstraction, in a language too recondite and too highly technical to appeal to a wider audience. In addition, most of them are of a polemic character. The attentive reader is forced to become personality-centered instead of problem-minded. Ethicists are notorious for faultfinding, for debunking theories on the basis of minute and subtle errors of inference. The result is that we learn more about failures of ethicists than about their achievements.

Since man began to think, the problem of good and evil has intrigued him. He has reflected on the issue very deeply and communicated his findings. There are profound insights and brilliant observations in the rich ethical literature. But there is no continuity of thought, no systematic body of knowledge. Small wonder that most people frown upon a scientific ethics with suspicion. The diversity and the polemic character of moral theories have encouraged many skeptics and relativists. An ethics which could be grounded in experience and commend itself to reason is for them a futile enterprise. For what reasons? Moral data, we are repeatedly told, are not perceptions, nor properties which can be studied objectively and experimented with, and our moral judgments, containing such terms as good, evil, right, and wrong, are more or less disguised emotive responses. Their real function is to persuade and not to inform, to goad to action and not to enlighten. After all, we are assured, the socially and culturally conditioned mentality of a thinker is at the root of his moral outlook, and not warranted cognitive data. This skeptical and relativistic approach to moral issues has a great appeal, not so much for the amount of truth it claims, as for the apparent comfort it offers. It nurtures our intellectual inertia. If skepticism is the final answer to the vexing issues of right and wrong, why waste time and energy on them?

There was a time, and not a too distant one, when similar skeptical voices were heard concerning our knowledge of nature. Claims to knowledge were vehemently discredited on various grounds—the subjectivity and fallibility of our senses, the limitations of our reason, the opaqueness of nature to man's aspirations, and what not. Even today when natural sciences can take justified pride in unique achievements, there are many people who disparage this pride. They discredit science for not revealing the true nature of things, their invariable essences or cosmic significance. Much of the ethical skepticism is of a similar character. We are bound to despair of finding solutions to moral problems if we are not clear as to the nature of the issues. If we expect from ethics an answer in terms of an ultimate, immutable good or right, a disclosure of principles of conduct true and valid independently of our bio-psychological make-up, such an ethics must fail, indeed. We do not know what an ultimate good is supposed to be, as little as we know what an ultimate truth is. And if we do not know what we are looking for, our quest is bound to be futile. But once we confine our task to what really perplexes us and diagnose issues properly, the chance for workable solutions in matters concerning morals are not less propitious than in matters studied by physics.

Ethicists are usually charged with dealing with a subject

matter for which there is no cumulative, empirically ascertained and valid knowledge. This sweeping accusation comes from many quarters: from natural scientists who mistrust data which defy any explanation or interpretation in mechanical, quantitative terms; from psychologists who believe that irrational impulses and desires govern man's behavior; from social scientists who eschew the problem of values or see in valuations mere individual or social idiosyncrasies; from politicians for whom brute expediency is the final standard of moral right, and from the host of contemporary semanticists and logicians who describe an ethical inquiry as a useless exercise in meaningless words.

To accept the belief in the noncumulative character of moral knowledge is to deny that there is any noticeable advance in our understanding of social and antisocial behavior. The most recalcitrant skeptic will be at a loss to prove that forms of aggression and cooperation are as inexplicable today as they were in the past. He may be able to show that some individuals or some social groups have not advanced above, or have even fallen below, the level of the savage in the jungle. Moral conduct may or may not improve, but ethical knowledge increases with any penetration into the intricate mechanism of human motivation, with any grasp of the sources of frustration and fulfillment, happiness, and misery.

The phrase of the noncumulative ethical knowledge rests to a certain extent with those ethicists who have unduly limited their inquiry to definitions and implications of a few concepts, blissfully forgetting that clarity of thought is the supreme requirement in dealing with any genuine philosophical problem, provided that logical vigor and lucidity of language do justice to the salient features of our moral experience which calls for elucidation. The problem of good and evil, right and wrong, is only partially a logical or semantic issue. To a larger extent it is a problem of brute actualities—hunger, suffering, humiliation, discrimination, deprivation of body and mind, overt and subtle aggressions, nurtured by social life. Semantic confusions are very often the driving forces behind social conflicts, but more frequently they are verbal, disguised surrogates of these conflicts. The existing class antagonisms, the material and spiritual deprivations, the narrowness of exclusive group participation, and the innumerable barriers which stand in the way of a full realization of our actual needs and ideal aspirations are the crucial elements behind man's tragic moral confusions.

The preoccupation with logical and linguistic analyses has blinded many ethicists to the essential moral problem, the conditions of the good life, which are in dire need of extensive studies. For men everywhere are more perplexed by the antecedent and consequent factors of the good life, or more ignorant of them than of the ambiguities of the moral language. It is not a clear definition of happiness, right, or justice that men want, but getting these values as realities, preserving and augmenting them.

The philosophical activities which comprise ethics have a threefold task: an integration of the empirical findings of the various studies of man; a clarification of the moral terms and their implications; and a projection of a feasible better state of affairs. These three tasks are interrelated. Ascertained knowledge is a necessary requirement for logical and semantic analyses. The latter in conjunction with verified propositions and tentative, meaningful hypotheses are the best guarantee against utopian visions, which either dwell on aspirations out of the context with reality or rationalize given conditions in a cryptic language. The zest for reform must be constantly checked against the background of experience and reason; otherwise it may mislead us to applaud the worse in the name of the better. The history of ethical reflection shows that these tasks have always been pursued. But very seldom have they been pursued simultaneously. Most ethicists have been preoccupied either with integration of available knowledge, or with logical elucidation, or with reconstruction. Logical clarity becomes a spurious value if the content is sacrificed for rigidity of form; a mass of facts is of little avail if the underlying concepts are vague; and any reconstruction which does not take into consideration the prevailing conditions—man's real limitations and opportunities—makes for regression rather than progress.

Whether justified or not, science may indulge in the comforting belief that it can pursue its objective without committing itself to certain values and norms of the better or worse; but moral philosophy can never resign itself to this value-neutrality. Ethical reflections do not stem from a detached contemplative attitude toward man's happiness and misery. They come from a deep sensitivity to man's weal and woe, from a fine grasp of the various conditions of the good life and the perpetual evils of injustice, abuse of power, poverty, and the aggressions man metes out to man. It is this noble sensitivity blended with deep observations and brilliant insights into the intricate complex of social behavior which makes ethical literature an abiding source of inspirations.

To understand human nature is the proper task of science. To dwell on man's possibilities for a better world is the proper domain of ethics. There are conflicting views among the great moral philosophers as to the salient features of our moral experience and the main conditions of the good life; but most of them agree as to the elements of the morally good life—a state of social affairs where misery is decreased, where ignorance and superstitions are replaced by knowledge and wisdom, where hatred is conquered by love, where discord makes room for accord, where conditions are favorable for peace and security, for cooperation and friendship, for growth and freedom. The ethicist shares with any genuine reformer the enthusiasm for the good life, but he differs from him in one important aspect. He avoids exhortations and panaceas which defy experience and reason. He does not hide the brute facts of life which make for strife and discord, but looks for means of mitigating them. Most of all, he encourages moral thinking, the most potent weapon in individual and social integration.

There are many valuable books which critically survey the diverse ethical theories, past and present. The following essays do not aim at such an exposition. The writer believes that an orientation by topics is the most suitable procedure to show the continual growth of moral ideas. A historically oriented account of the main ethical systems makes us lose sight of the vital issues and focus our attention more on the expounder of a theory, than on its merits and demerits. Synoptic views, envisaged and elaborated by single thinkers, are likely to contain a strange mixture of warranted knowledge and sweeping generalizations, valid conclusions and glaring inconsistencies. By keeping a lively interest in the problem itself we may cultivate that kind of criticism which has been very fruitful in the natural sciences, constructive criticism. In philosophy too often the prevailing attitudes are still edifying and disparaging. Hence the numerous repetitious expositions of a given system of ideas or the endless faultfinding analyses. In the natural sciences an unworkable hypothesis is rejected; in philosophy it is revived in order to be discarded again and again.

CHAPTER I

HUMAN NATURE AND NURTURE

"Give a dog a bad name and hang him." "Human nature has been the dog of professional moralists, and consequences accord with the proverb. Man's nature has been regarded with suspicion, with fear, with sour looks, sometimes with enthusiasm for its possibilities, but only when these were placed in contrast with its actualities. It has appeared to be so evilly disposed that the business of morality was to prune and curb it; it would be thought better of if it could be replaced by something else." [1]

Moral pessimists have a ready-made answer to the ubiquity of man's aggressiveness, to the perennial social discords on the national and international scene, to the high incidence of crime, the overt acts of violence and the more subtle, covert forms of destructiveness: the innate, irrational, unalterable pugnacity of human nature. Empirical, unbiased studies disprove the doctrine of an unalterable, aggressive human nature. We learn that social aggressiveness is an acquired trait of a very complex character and of multiple causation. Socio-cultural factors are decisive. Many forms of aggressiveness are results of frustrations, emotional fixation or regression, of adherence to outdated ways of reaction, known as cultural lag.

To explain the recurrent acts of barbarism, crime and war on the basis of an innate, destructive urge or death instinct (Freud) is to fail in distinguishing the array of natural impulses and passions and the forms acquired through the process of socialization and culturation. Man would not fight without an innate impulse or passion. But the same impulse or passion which becomes hostility may under proper conditions turn into amity. The same impulse which develops into suspicion, distrust, may become mutual trust and respect.[2] The need for affection may be crippled by being confined to a small group, with hatred to man at large, or may develop into a most pervasive and most sensitive attitude to human misery and happiness. The urge for novelty and adventure may be channeled into art or science, or into the most inhuman or subhuman treatment of the fellow men. The socialization and humanization of native impulses and passions is the result of training, education and learning. The human infant is not moral or immoral, rather amoral. He becomes moral or immoral in the course of years by interacting with various environmental forces which determine his love and hatred, loyalty and disloyalty, constructive or destructive interests and goals.

If we reflect upon the undeniable fact that no child is born with prejudices of any kind—national, racial, or religious—with no hatred toward other persons, with no conceit based on the many pseudo-values as to origin and status, we grasp the unpleasant truth that the evil men heap upon men is their own creation. It is nurture and not nature that perpetuates man's ignorance, bias, aggressiveness, the insatiable lust for power, and lust to kill. The readiness with which men everywhere respond to destructive aims suggests an innate, pugnacious impulse as long as we take it as a final datum. In reality it is not an ultimate, inexplicable fact. This readiness is a result of a long series of deprivations and frustrations.

Beliefs in innate pugnacity of man and an innate sociability of man are not true to fact. A proper evaluation of the vast variety of social behavior—from aggressiveness to cooperation, from peaceful coexistence to brutal extermination, from trust to violent mistrust—points to the great plasticity of man's natural, amoral endowment. The relatively scant number of native, undifferentiated impulses and drives, so highly indicative of man, is not something to repine about if we focus our attention on the unique human asset: man's educational possibilities. No other creature is as trainable and educable as man. The plasticity of human nature does not support the major assertion of ethical and cultural relativism that man may be conditioned to any way of life which may have the same degree of satisfaction. Conditioned ways of life differ as to their moral value in promoting or stifling, gratifying or frustrating man's basic and derivative needs in the ongoing struggle for survival and enhancement of life.

The greatest obstacle to a harmonious social life, to a life of abundance and fulfillment, is not the hidden beast in man, but rather the inertia of social customs and institutions which disregard blatant facts related to man's needs and mainsprings of action. There is no denial that our scientific outlook finds no counterpart in our moral outlook. Sociologists call it cultural lag, a phenomenon we encounter in every society, primitive as well as more advanced ones. But this cultural lag need not be perpetuated once we realize that it is not an outgrowth of an unalterable human nature. The unalterability of human nature is a myth invented and adhered to by people who hide their selfish interests behind the sanctity of an outworn tradition. Slavery, caste system, feudal serfdom, discrimination, inequality of races, wars are not grounded in a primordial, pugnacious human nature. They are rooted in customs and institutions which employ innate capacities to promote and foster social discord. "History does not prove the inevitability of war, but it does prove that customs and institutions which organize native powers into certain patterns in politics and economics will also generate the war-pattern." [3]

The regularities and diversities of human behavior have three interdependent sources: biological, physical, and social or cultural. Except for reflexes and behavior under great physiological strain, no human being acts as a mere biological organism. He usually behaves as a bio-social being. His hereditary capacities to respond to various situations are constantly influenced by social and cultural factors. He does not face a situation in a pristine way. His reactions are circumscribed within various cultural patterns out of which he internalized a specific part, mediated and transmitted by particular parents, a specific community, and social roles he plays. The kind of environment with which we interact is decisive in the rate and quality of our growth, intellectual, emotional, and social. Being thrust into a world of ever-changing conditions, our inborn dispositions, instincts, reflexes, drives, and homeostatic processes, in short, our biological endowment could not suffice in our struggle for survival, still less in our endeavor to secure and enhance life. We succeed as social beings. In all probability a more potent agent than sympathy in the process of socialization and humanization has been the brute exigencies of living—the innumerable destructive natural forces which threaten existence, the wild beast preying upon us, and our prolonged infancy. The effects of socialization are twofold: the alleviation of the struggle for the necessities of living by an increased mastery over nature, due to the accumulated, cooperative wisdom, and the diminution of fear of aggression from other men. This is the essence of any genuine culture which is man's addition to nature, selective, successful ways of reacting to, and changing of, the given environment. Man has succeeded in diminution of fear of nature. He is less successful in diminution of fear of man by man.[4]

No other study abounds in so many dichotomies as the study of man. Just to mention a few wide-spread divisions: the individual and society, freedom and authority, reason and emotions, heredity and environment, and many more. These antithetical distinctions are results of one-sided analyses and interpretations of man's existence. They have in common a tendency toward oversimplifications and ignoring or sidetracking difficult problems. Such artificial dichotomies appeal to our inveterate inertia which keeps us away from patient observation of facts and projection of bold hypotheses, the two indispensable requirements in the process of acquiring warranted knowledge. The above-mentioned disjunctions are in reality meaningless. We cannot separate the individual from society, or society from the individual. The same holds true of the other dichotomies. Freedom apart from order or authority is nonexistent. The untenable division between heredity and environment, nature and culture reflects idiosyncrasies of single individuals or groups. The exclusively hereditary approach mirrors an aristocratic bias for a status quo; the environmental approach in turn reveals the mentality of people who would like to blame given institutions or social forces for their own moral deviations.

Man is a joint product of heredity and environment, or nature and nurture, which constantly interact. No human trait or characteristic is entirely hereditary or entirely environmental, but rather the result of innate capacities modified by environmental forces. Absolutely fixed or absolutely modifiable traits are fictitious; we have only relatively fixed and relatively plastic traits. The relatively fixed characteristics comprise our physiological make-up in the form of mental capacity, reflexes, texture and color of the hair, constitutional strength or weakness, and the most general temperamental traits described as greater or weaker activity or passivity. Relatively flexible and plastic characteristics are our social or antisocial attitudes, our likes or dislikes, derivative motives or behavior designated as social needs, differentiated sensitivities and canalized interests. The controversy as to the primary importance of heredity or environment is futile, for man always behaves as a bio-social organism with a congenital endowment and an environment acting upon it. Heredity as a distinct entity or environment as a separate entity are fictitious constructions.

Social and cultural variables operate within and through a certain biological structure which is common to all men. To neglect these common traits is to embrace a very out-dated concept of the human mind as a tabula rasa (Locke). Environmental determinants explain a great deal of man's social behavior, but not everything. There are certain invariant features of human existence which are not affected by social or cultural factors. The almost universal emotional syndromes of rivalry, jealousy, inferiority rest more on the biological helplessness of the child than on a specific enculturation.

Behind the diverse socially and culturally conditioned ways of response and adjustment there are common elements which have their roots in man's common biological and psychological substratum. The socio-cultural variability may easily blind us to the latter if we focus our attention on food habits, etiquette, artistic and religious activities, family and economic institutions. But once we concentrate on the few intrinsic ends of life men everywhere aspire to, universal transcultural elements become clearly discernible —parental love, care of children, division of labor, the urge to explore, regulations of conduct, the need for giving and receiving affection and the sense of belonging. No culture has ever made suffering into a desirable good. No society "fails to put a negative valuation upon killing, indiscriminate lying and stealing within the in-group." [5]

The major neuroses and psychoses take the same general form regardless of the socio-economic conditions. The etiology of crime is the same, although some specific causes may be more predominant in one culture than in another. Various cultures may employ different devices in transforming the amoral infant into a mature social and moral being, but the intensity and duration of the moral feelings and beliefs depend upon common psychological agents and laws governing the process of maturation. The limitations and opportunities of socialization and humanization vary from individual to individual, but not from nation to nation, or culture to culture. The course of human growth points to intercultural categories—self-appreciation or self-depreciation, ego-enclosure or ego-expansion, repression, sublimation, projection, and rationalization.

The widespread belief that culture, the sum total of acquired ways of satisfying needs, of adaptation to, and changing external situations, the invention of language, art, religion, and science are mere additions to, or superimposed on, an unchangeable biological human nature, is not true to fact. The biological and cultural humaneness are inseparable entities which continuously interact. The acquired ways of acting may be in accord or discord with biological human nature, the product of a long evolutionary process.[6]

Our biological nature is not an unalterable entity, or a clay to be molded or conditioned to any possible cultural design. To a certain extent it is less rigid than entrenched cultural responses, practices, and mores. Culture, as a rule, has greater refractoriness to change than our biological impulses, needs, and passions.[7] Although breaking through the rigidity of culture and its inertia is a difficult task, man has the unique gift of resisting anachronistic ways of life, of fighting entrenched forces which cripple his potentialities or arrest growth. "It is just as human to fight against cultural standardization as it is to submit to it; and, under conditions of modern living, the creative forces of curiosity and of artistic and scientific reorganization of the materials and ways of life may over-power many of the massive conservative forces of culture. This creative thrust of understanding is a third human nature." [8]

The individual is culturally conditioned. His standards of right and wrong reflect traditional determinants acting upon him. But he also is able to influence the cultural environment. The fact that he can discern the many wrongs in the same social habitat disproves the main tenet of social relativism, that a given society validates the right and wrong. Our moral outlooks are certainly more static than our interpretations of nature, but by no means as stationary as cultural relativists would have us believe. Whenever we move from one set of values to another one, it is not some mysterious entity called society which does the appraisal. It is always single individuals who because of a greater sensitivity to human misery and better knowledge bring an advance about. [9]

Individual creativity transcends cultural and social boundaries. It attests the undeniable fact that man is much more than a mere reflection of cultural forces. Morals aim at control of human nature. Their success and failure depend upon their functions in bringing about harmony or disharmony between the native impulses or drives and the social and cultural demands or exigencies of a cooperative communal life. Man's natural impulses are very plastic. Our adjustment to the changing physical environment is a function of this plasticity. Our adjustment to the changing social environment, although not as successful as to the physical environment, points to vital social impulses which make for living together. Since no human being can live for and by himself, some of man's basic needs are social. Living together makes us want and pursue things beyond a mere subsistence level; the needs for self-respect, for social status, for prestige, for affection are as genuine as hunger.

Cultural anthropology calls our attention to the impact of

social forces on our ways of perceiving, thinking, and acting. By describing this process merely in terms of the social context, it disregards the basic drives which may be expressed or inhibited in the various cultural settings. If we accept the extreme sociological view, the biological determinants of behavior become irrelevant, which they are not. If we accept the extreme naturalistic or physiological view, the enculturating process leaves man's basic needs intact, which it does not. The relatively few physiological needs and impulses and the great number of socially elaborate motives must be viewed in their vital interaction where none is supreme. Findings guard us against hasty accentuation of one aspect of reality at the price of another one. "Why should not the pattern of social interaction, like 'leadership' or 'imitation' be conceived as expressions of an underlying motivation, impossible without the energy to which the term motivation refers, but cast in a socially defined form? Just as magnetized iron may itself become magnet, so love, etc. may be both intrinsically determined and socially determined. Social behavior becomes a socially patterned release of inherent energies."[10]

Since empirical studies of man are, relatively speaking, new, the most common interpretations of human nature fall into the category of doctrines, dogmatic, speculative assertions, pessimistic or optimistic projections, fatalistic or indeterminate explanations, cyclical or progressive designs, and what not. They all have in common generalizations beyond empirical evidence, hasty conclusions, instances of false causation, begging the question, speculative arguments and the like. In spite of many brilliant insights into man's potentialities, the Greek view is essentially a metaphysical one. It interprets man's essence as dormant cognitive tendencies and goals which given environments may fulfill or frustrate, but never engender or modify. The Hebrew-Christian doctrine, very much alike to all major living religions, views man as a depraved creature, full of imperfections and unable to find self-fulfillment without the grace of a divine power. Suffering, misery, and deprivations are accepted as just events, visitations upon man because of his sinful, corrupt nature. This pessimistic evaluation of man has found forceful exponents in Hobbes, in Schopenhauer, and in the classical economists of the 19th century, for whom man is a selfish being, motivated exclusively by the profit incentive; in the disciples of Darwin who predicate man's survival upon his aggressive impulses; in Freud, who in addition to libido, accepts a second innate urge of self-destructive and social pugnacity; in a vast number of contemporary psychologists and sociologists, for whom man's nonrational endowment is most essential.

Not less untenable is the optimistic view of man, which has found in Rousseau a classical representative. According to him, human nature is essentially social, cooperative, free from all the overt and covert forms of aggressiveness that civilization engenders and fosters. Rousseau's notion of the good, noble savage is a myth. Nowhere do we find such a creature. Rousseau notwithstanding, civilization is mainly responsible for man's conquest of savagery. On a precultural level, man lacks any genuine freedom of growth. His life, partly licentious, partly curbed by all kinds of irrational taboos, is fixated and arrested, constantly driven by fear, the most destructive emotion from the point of view of individual self-realization and social cohesion. Rousseauian return to nature is the least desirable ideal.

In the light of the growing information from the various sciences, physiological, psychological and social, man's nature must be viewed as having potentialities for good and evil, for aggression and cooperation, for constructive and destructive tendencies and habits. Man is neither good nor bad, but both; neither gregarious nor solitary, but both;

neither selfish nor altruistic, but both. This twofold nature of man makes morality an unending task, to be fulfilled only by approximation. To assume that man may become totally moral is to indulge in utopian wishes. But man may become more moral, more social, more considerate once we find ways and techniques to channel native impulses and desires into socially desirable patterns. The best way to make man into a moral being is to have moral injunctions more congenial to man's nature, to make them into a source of enduring satisfaction.

As to the kind of potentialities we ought to promote, this depends on what kind of morality we desire to implement. To claim that all potentialities have an equal right to fulfillment is to take an amoral view. An ethics which aspires to be a critical appraisal of given moral practices and beliefs cannot help subscribing to basic value presuppositions as a priori commitments. These value commitments are: human life is worthy of preservation; a life of happiness and abundance is preferable to a life of misery and deprivation; cooperation and security are better than a life of struggle and violence. Once we accept these value presuppositions, which articulate the cherished values of the vast majority of people everywhere, the choice between better and worse potentialities becomes a rational one. Conflict is a concomitant feature of life, but man does not cherish conflict as an intrinsic end. Men struggle to mitigate conflict. Potentialities whose fulfillment leads to satisfaction should be given wider scope than potentialities which increase frustrations, intra-psychic and interpersonal conflicts. The final test as to the desirable potentialities is man's enduring gratification. Empirical findings prove that general affection and sensitivity to the joys and sorrows of other people are essential for one's own happiness. Social feelings enrich our interests, widen our horizons, keep our ideals and goals alive. They liberate and sublimate our impulses and passions in two areas of social living—curiosity and love. "It seems that only a studied blindness could make us unaware that it is good for the soul of man to be curious, to be inquiring, to seek answers, just as it is joyful to love persons and be loved by them."[11]

CHAPTER II

MORAL CONDUCT

Character and conduct are complementary units. Habits, dispositions, feelings, conations, cognitions and the ensuing acts are conjoined as interdependent parts of the moral and immoral phenomena. Although the consequences of behavior are often accidental, beyond our foresight and control, dispositions, motives, and intentions are not moral or immoral unless they are objectified in deeds. We do not praise benevolence and condemn malice as mere states of mind or will, but rather as traits which manifest themselves in concrete actions.

Moral traits are dispositions to act. Without constant employment and reemployment in concrete situations their effectiveness decreases. Apart from certain tendencies to act in accordance with fitting and obligatory situations, virtues and vices are nonexistent. There is no morality or immorality of the good or bad man who does not cause the good and evil in reality. Deeds cannot be appraised as detached from dispositions, nor character traits apart from their ascertained consequences. Occasional disparities between motives and intentions and the outcome of the act are common. But a persisting gap between these two is a reliable indication that our appraisal of the moral character has been a hasty one. Making a proper allowance for unforeseen accidents in our moral conduct, a thorough scrutiny of both the outcome of the act and the dispositions of the agent is the best guarantee against rash approval and disapproval, praise and condemnation.

The occasional disparities between man's character and the outcome of his actions prompted many ethicists to move from one extreme to another one. The accidental consequence of an act inspired Kant's ethical formalism, which rules out inclinations and the resulting gratifications in appraising the moral and immoral behavior. For Kant only the good will is eminently ethical, a will prompted and guided by the moral law which enjoins us to apply the test of universality. According to him, we act morally if we act on the principle of the categorical imperative ("Act in conformity with that maxim, and that maxim only, which you can at the same time will to be a universal law").

This emphasis on the will acting on principles, Kant shares with many ethicists who derive man's morality from his rational being. But man's being cannot be separated from his acting, which may leave the total situation better or worse, may increase the amount of happiness or misery of other sentient people. It is not generosity as a state of mind or will which is moral, but a generosity which eventuates in doing things conducive to man's quest for an enduring satisfaction. Neither do we acclaim kindness as a character trait without its consequences in reality, but rather kindness which increases the good things in life.

Just as an undue stress on inner states of mind fails to do justice to moral and immoral phenomena, similarly an undue stress on an act fails to do it. Social hedonists or utilitarians (such as Bentham, Mill) overstress the consequences of an act. Consequences not attributable to the agent are amoral. Consequences appraised as moral or immoral flow from man's specific character, from his cognitive grasp of the total situation, from his foresight based on available knowledge, and will effort to implement what appears as a moral requiredness of a given situation.

Moral acts in which we relate ourselves to our fellow men are voluntary, purposive acts. Learning and unlearning are the essential features of purposive conduct. Acts appraised morally are predicated on man's freedom of choice among various alternative courses of action. Such a freedom is not freedom from determinants. We could never choose under the assumption of an undetermined or indifferent will. It is the kind of determinants which is decisive in our freedom. Pressures of immediate circumstances, physical and psychological restraints, ignorance of the consequences of an act, blind passions detached from cognitions, emotional fixation and perseverance which fancy their object or impute to it characteristics which are not given in reality—these are the vital impediments to freedom, which is in essence freedom from action-limiting, interests-crippling, goals-frustrating, and growth-impeding conditions. In making a man morally responsible we are looking for determinants which narrow or widen his range of choices.

Moral conduct is predicated on choice. Ethical reflections center on the right course of action. Because our desires, interests, and goals conflict, we need inquiries into situations which confront us, a clarification of their requiredness, an imaginary rehearsal of the possible consequences of the contemplated act, and an evaluation of the decision in the light of the feasibility of ends to which we commit ourselves. "Wide sympathy, keen sensitiveness, persistence in the face of the disagreeable, balance of interests enabling us to undertake the work of analysis and decision intelligently are distinctively moral traits—the virtues of moral excellence."[1] Choice is not occurrence at random. It has antecedents and consequences. It draws from our fund of experiences as well as from experiences of other people. It is a matter of character, of the given opportunities, and pressures within the social and cultural environment. It has its roots in our habits, sentiments, attitudes, and cognitive beliefs. In choosing there is not a subject endowed with a mysterious free will and a causally determined world, but an interaction of the two equally determined entities. The choice we praise or condemn, approve or disapprove is not an undetermined choice, a choice without motives, intentions, projected and executed actions, but a choice flowing from certain motives and intentions, enriched by or deprived of foresight. Our native nature supplies the raw material of the choice—the impulses, desires, interests. The way they interact with the various environments is decisive for its moral or immoral quality.

Choice is a matter of habits, the acquired ways of acting. Without habits there would be mere acting on impulses or a distracting hesitation. As in thinking so in acting habits make for connection of discrete units, for familiarity of facts, for the necessary hold in facing new situations. No moral injunction could get hold of us without habits. In deliberations we do not look for inducements to act. These are given in our desires and passions, in the countless deficiencies and blockings of the given situation. The habits point in the direction of satisfying, consummatory experiences. The formation of habits, desirable as well as undesirable, obeys the law of success. As a child develops and perseveres in temper tantrums because of their adjustive function in getting attention, so the juvenile and the adult criminal develop antisocial habits because at one time or another these ways of acting have been rewarded. A sound training in morality must take care that social behavior finds satisfaction, antisocial conduct dissatisfaction.

Choice is a matter of intelligence not in the sense of innate capabilities but in the sense of a mature, fully developed reason. An intelligent choice is an informed one, nurtured constantly by warranted knowledge related to the exigencies of social relations. Impulses and desires urge to action, intelligence guides it in the light of anticipated consequences and the unique requiredness of a perplexing situation. Intelligent deliberation in conjunction with the appropriate feelings places the desire in its widest context and cautions it against blind imputing of values.

Choice does not occur in a moral vacuum. It mirrors a world where good and evil are actualities. Fulfillments and frustrations, enjoyments and sufferings are data which call for moral reflection and deliberation. A choice which enriches the good life is conditioned by the good life. No exhortation to moral virtues is of any noticeable avail in an environment where these virtues find no satisfaction. There is no better, no more rational way of bringing about a high moral order than taking care that this order can be appreciated, enjoyed, and desired. Intelligence does not cause the appreciation of the good things in life. It enhances it. The desire for the good and aversion against the evil comes after enjoyment of the good and suffering from the evil. A moral choice is predicated on actualities of a moral world.

Moral conduct is acting on principles. Comparative ethics knows of "no pre-moral stage, that is of any societies where there are no rules, upheld by the general judgment of the people, distinguishing between what may or may not be done. If there has been a development of morals, it has been a development in this the field of morality and not a development of morals out of something else."[2] Necessities of life call for social groupings. Apart from his prolonged infancy, man's total existence depends upon the cooperative efforts of many in procuring food, shelter, clothing, protection against nature as well as human aggressions. His social existence is not only a biological exigency. It is also a psychological necessity. Man has a need to share his joys and sorrows. He has an intense fear of the unknown, finds himself bewildered in contemplating the vastness of the universe, and is tormented by a gnawing consciousness of finitude, sickness and death. Anguish and despair are concomitants of living which would be unbearable but for the lively echo we find in other people of our anxieties and exaltations, joys and griefs. Living together, sharing a common lot, make for a vital catharsis of deeply depressing emotions, by liberating positive feelings of compassion, love and friendliness. Happy social relatedness is probably the most cherished feature of the good life. "Human beings outside society can live only the most primitive animal-like lives. They have no chance of achieving a full satisfying life. Without education, without language, without a cultural heritage to draw on, without the division of labor, without skills, without an ordered and settled way of life, existence is a continuous struggle against nature, leaving no time for any of the things that are most worth while."[3]

Genuine, ethical controversies focus on the nature of moral principles, on their rationality and feasibility, and not on such questions of a mere academic character as "why be moral?" which amounts to asking "Why live in society?" Fortunately for the human race, only criminals, selfish leeches challenge the benefits of a moral life. For the vast majority of people everywhere it is the immoral behavior which calls for a justification, and not the moral.[4]

The choice concerning morals is not one of being moral or immoral. It is a choice between rational and nonrational moral principles; between parochial and universal rules of conduct; between the spurious moral right which disguises individual and group interests and the moral right which answers to the needs of men everywhere; between standards which commend themselves to reason and coercive, hypocritical standards. Man's history of experimenting in living together has led to rules of conduct whose efficacy for the common good is beyond question. The very existence of communal life is contingent upon adherence to them. The injunctions not to kill not to harm, the golden rule "don't do unto others as you would not have them do unto you" are time-tested rules. To challenge them is to question man's social existence. Unfortunately, man is still blinded to their universal character and follows them in a tribalistic spirit. Man's intellectual inertia in matters of morality is too obvious to labor on. It prevents him from finding better means to control human nature in the light of social exigencies. It makes us look upon nature as an inherent evil and opaque to reason or as an inherent goodness spoiled and corrupted by civilization. The severing of morals from their physiological, psychological, and social contexts accounts for many common fallacies: that good and evil are subjective opinions or socially sanctioned approvals and disapprovals; that moral values are superimposed on a value-neutral human nature; that ethical injunctions have a transcendent origin, and what not. The disregard of the vital continuity of nature, man and society has led to a romantic glorification of the natural state of man (Rousseau), to a preoccupation with moral values as perfect nontemporal entities (Plato), or as ideals foreign to human nature.

There would be no need for ethics if our self-realization were always harmonious with the self-realization of other people, if the interests of single individuals coincided with the interests of society at large. Neither could any ethics prevail if there were a complete disparity between both. Our interests and desires harmonize and conflict. Hence an ethics of self-interest (no matter how enlightened it may be) must be supplemented by an ethics of duties and obligations. Only such a completion can diminish conflicts and discords. The success or failure of moralities depends on whether or not they avail themselves of the warranted knowledge related to man's social behavior or continue to rationalize aggressiveness as an innate, unalterable trait.

The diversity of moral practices and moral terms need not make us despair of a universal ethos, for such a diversity may disguise basic human values. Psychoanalytic studies prove that our verbal assertions about our likes and dislikes, the important and unimportant, the desirable and undesirable do not, of necessity, reveal our true valuations. To ascertain them we must grope deeper, we must study man's total conduct as it flows from his conscious and unconscious life. The moral language we employ may be socially and culturally conditioned; not so our intrinsic values. Men everywhere crave for the good things in life, the satisfaction of innate as well as derivative needs, but a given society may cover up its inability to procure such gratifications by disparaging the needs themselves and sanction norms of conduct which put emphasis on sacrifice, inhibition, and curtailment. Ethical relativists and skeptics fail to grasp that verbalizations concerning the good things in life are not always true reports. "The ascetic who claims to value self-inflicted starvation and mutilation is taken to be an accurate reporter concerning his own psychical processes. But verbal reports are notorious for their untruthfulness, for their failure to penetrate to underlying levels of the personality. In reporting his values, the person is only too apt to state what he has been taught he ought to state."[5]

Man's total behavior, his joys and sorrows, his expectations and aspirations are a more reliable clue to his values than his linguistic articulations. The good life we experience defies the widespread beliefs in the discontinuity of nature and morals, in the dichotomy of material and spiritual values. A neglect of material values makes us immune to the beauty of spiritual values. A neglect of spiritual values reduces human existence to the level of an animal. A morality rises with the gratification of all values. Enduring social bonds are contingent upon such a fulfillment.

The social context of valuations and values is no evidence against an objective ethics. The latter subscribes to the rational belief that there are features of the good life, distinctive ties and consummatory effects of social relations which answer to human needs and aspirations. No particular social sanctioning or conditioning can obscure them in the long run. Just as our beliefs about nature, no matter how socially and culturally conditioned they might be, have undergone a change from irrationalisms to rationalism, from arbitrary opinions to warranted assertions, so too, similar changes do occur in our moral outlook. This change, no doubt, is much slower. Every society shows a discrepancy between the scientific conceptual framework of nature and the social, moral, political outlook, customs, entrenched power interests, and superstitions perpetuate. It is the dimension of this gap which is decisive for rationality of morals.

The diversity of moral outlooks of the vast civilized population is more apparent than real. Here we find that cannibalism, incest, human sacrifice, promiscuity, exposure of children to cruel treatment, unqualified killing, arbitrary justice and arbitrary assessment of guilt are things of the past, unless we accept their occasional, sporadic appearances as a justified case for a moral relativism. The vicious criminal who deceives, lies, tortures and kills is certainly not the case for ethical subjectivism or relativism. Neither are the numerous tyrants who make a mockery of human justice and dignity. One need not be a member of a particular culture or society to respond with horror to their crimes. It is our emotional and intellectual maturity which makes us realize the oneness of the human race, its common needs and values. The bloody political arena of the past and present makes all values a matter of transient expediency. Not so the population at large, in whom a common humanity is a living force which is being obscured, argued away by men driven by an insatiable lust for power. Human history has been dreadful because of divisive, irrational beliefs spread by mentally sick and morally deranged people.

We hear so often that from the fact that men want to

live, that they aspire to a happy, satisfying life, does not follow that they have a right to these values. The justification of human rights has been a subject of futile controversies, not because there are no such rights, but rather because we do not know what such a justification ought to be. Rights are asserted needs. Upon the recognition of such rights depends organized, communal life. A man who refuses to recognize the needs of other people puts himself behind the requirements of a civilized society. It is not the recognition of human rights which is in need of a justification but the refusal of such a recognition. People who challenge the basic rights of other people are in dire need of moral training; they are certainly no subjects for an ethical discourse. They lack the most basic requirements for such a discourse: the basic humane feelings, and insights that our own rights entail obligations toward other people. The recognition of human rights is not a function of our perceptive abilities, for rights are not sensed properties of objects; neither is it a function of a discursive reasoning, for moral conclusions must contain moral premises. It is the result of training in, and an intelligent grasp of, the various exigencies of living together.

That human happiness is an end worthy of being cultivated is the basic axiological commitment of the vast majority of ethicists. Without this commitment moral controversies turn into sophisticated linguistic and logical analyses. What has given rise to the current skeptical and relativistic trend is the belief that there are no objective criteria of human happiness, that man's bio-psychological and bio-social nature can be conditioned and reconditioned arbitrarily. The diverse moral practices and codes seem to support such a view, but only if we fail to investigate the actual well-being of man under the various social and cultural conditions. It is true that man may endure a life of extreme deprivation, but he will not cherish such a life as a desirable goal; he may be conditioned to an existence full of hatred and animosity toward the near and remote fellow men, but the crippling of his affective life will make him unhappy; he may learn to renounce the joyful things in life and acclaim suffering, but his repressed drives will play havoc with his conscious and subconscious self.

An objective ethics subscribes to the normative distinction between the better and worse, the right and wrong of moral practices and beliefs. The standard is rationality and workability. Norms of conduct may be decreed arbitrarily without due regard to the human nature which they intend to control. Such rules of behavior achieve the opposite of what they intend to accomplish. Instead of social cohesion and harmony they generate discord and disorganization. Moral principles which could effect a better society cannot be posited at will. They must be discovered by a patient, unbiased study of the various causes of social accord and discord. The "ought" they articulate and epitomize must come from ascertained facts of social interaction. Where transgressions of the moral ought prevail over conforming, there, too, is an indication that the moral ought does not flow from human nature. The transition from facts to norms, from descriptive to prescriptive statements is not the domain of the theoretical, discursive reason. It is the proper function of the practical reason which guides our conduct upon warranted knowledge. Science shows us the connection between frustration and aggression, the oughtness which tells us to diminish frustrations is a basic feature of reason in conduct. Its obligatoriness rests on our conative nature, on our desires, goals, and aspirations.

CHAPTER III

THE PLACE OF EMOTIONS IN CONDUCT

Emotion or feeling is probably the most complex physiological and psychological phenomenon. Small wonder that we have a variety of definitions and descriptions of emotions. The most common are: emotion is an unconscious conation; emotion is a psychic agitation; emotion is a conscious motivation; emotion is a pattern of organic response; emotion is a disturbance manifest in aimless behavior.[1] These various descriptions are complementary. They accentuate different qualities of the very pervasive elements called emotions. The available knowledge proves that feelings are intimately fused with conations and cognitions. In a normal human being we cannot separate attitudes and feelings from their wider matrix of perceptions, beliefs, and goals. Feelings are aroused by external and internal stimuli, by apprehending specific qualities of the surrounding environment, by visceral changes, and by the memory of past experiences.

The salient feature of emotions is their pervasiveness. Feelings play a vital role in our ongoing interaction with the various environments, physical and social. Contemporary psychiatry explains mild and severe maladjustments as a result of emotional fixation, repression, retrogression, and projection. Not only mental health, but also to a high degree physiological health is contingent upon proper emotions. We learn more and more about feelings as the major causes of psychosomatic diseases. Emotional factors are involved in metabolic and endocrine disturbances, in skin diseases, in respiratory, gastrointestinal, cardiovascular, and joint ailments.

With the exception of a few emotions (fear, rage, love in its rudimentary forms) most emotional responses are learned. We acquire emotional habits the same way we acquire other habits: through trial and error, opportunity, guidance, imitation, success or reward. As we mature, our emotions undergo a change from diffused to specific behavior, from violent to controlled and articulate expressions. Emotional maturity shows a correlation between perceiving, willing, thinking, and feeling. Emotional immaturity lacks such correspondence. It exhibits fixated, arrested emotional habits.

The physiology of emotions is well known. We understand the various organic reactions emotions bring about—the change in the bodily temperature, the increase or decrease of the pulse rate, perspiration, breathing rate, the change in glandular functions, etc. There is an intimate link between our visceral organs and emotional reactions. Emotionally aroused individuals display highly agitated visceral activities which are "not directly responsive to or regulated by the immediate local visceral conditions. Thus vomiting in response to irritative gastric contents we do not consider an emotional reaction, but vomiting induced by bad news we do." [2] The pervasive influence of strong feelings stems from the fact that our visceral organs once activated may persist without external stimulation. The same fact explains emotional displacement and cumulative emotional tensions highly incongruent with reality. Persisting strong emotions are a great hindrance in our daily tasks and social relations. As transitory occurrences they have adjustive value, especially when unusual bodily performances are needed, e.g. facing dangerous situations or any competitive sport performance.

The bodily strength of such emotions is due to their inhibition of digestive processes, which inhibitions release blood to our extremities.

The psychology of emotions trails behind the physiology of emotions for the apparent reason of dealing with conscious states of mind which require a great deal of trained introspection. It is easier to record observable data which command consensus than to deal with covert entities whose elucidation is bound up with many inferential assertions and hypothetical constructions, the acceptance of which is less obligatory. Nevertheless, there is a convergence of views that feelings are not separate entities apart from other psychic functions. Emotion is interpreted as an accompanying element of other psychic processes. Whether we experience anger or gratitude, hostility or amity, fear or calmness, our feelings have a perceptive and cognitive basis, they are object-bound. Feelings make us dwell on perceived events which have a beneficial or harmful effect upon us. They are "modes to detect the signification of situations, to know what is savory, disgusting, alarming, distressing, lovely, etc." [3] Common feelings show a congruence with reality. To fear a situation which is not dangerous is to reveal a trait of oneself. Fear of a threatening object or event is a shareable experience. Feeling and thinking are "biologically inseparable" [4] The felt estimate of a situation and our cognitive appraisal are complementary. Feelings engender cognitions, and cognitions in turn influence emotions by attaching them to objects and goals worthy of pursuit. "Just as there are true ideas and false ideas, so it may be said that there are true feelings and false feelings. I do not intend this in a moral sense; I mean rather that some feelings have a true sort of understanding and others a false. The former have a sense of reality and adapt themselves to it, whereas the latter go contrary to their own ends, and act inconsistently." [5]

Our emotional responses to given stimuli are not pristine. They are determined by previous experiences and social and cultural factors. The latter work on both levels, conscious and unconscious. Emotions mediate between ourselves and given environments. They tell a great deal about both. The close ego-relatedness of feelings have blinded many people to the role of emotions in the process of disclosing specific traits of objects and events. Even the most recalcitrant advocate of the subjectivity of emotions must admit a mental derangement of persons responding with joy to sad situations or with sorrow to joyful situations. Education in moral values is predicated on common emotive experiences. No moral injunction could be of any avail if men did not share basic joys and sorrows.

The distinction between normal and abnormal emotional responses is predicated on their relatedness or unrelatedness to reality. Like perceptions, emotions refer to ascertained objective data. Both are selective functions. Any given environment comprises more than we perceive or feel. Neither perceptions nor emotions copy the real. They dwell on those aspects of reality which relate to our needs, goals, and aspirations. What makes perceptions and emotions normal is their object-directed nature. When they lose the representational characteristics, when the interaction between the organism and its environment is distorted or interrupted, perceptions turn into hallucinations, while emotions become blind, chaotic subjective responses, highly incongruent with reality. The objects and events to which emotions refer in their normal functioning are not entities unrelated to our needs, and motives. They are biologically and socially relevant data, pregnant with meanings, derived from past experiences and enriched by new ones. The state of mind they express is an intentional consciousness, a consciousness aware of reality. Feelings make us look for values and disvalues, the pleasant and unpleasant, fulfilling and frustrating situations. They do not constitute the value aspects of objects and events. They make us aware of them.

Feelings unchecked by perceptual data become private, non-shareable responses. The same holds true of emotions unchecked by proper ideas and beliefs. Fear, anxiety, joy, and sorrow without any basis in verified cognitions are strong indicators of mild or severe mental deviations. In a healthy individual emotions detached from cognitions are rare phenomena. Love without warranted and corrigible knowledge of the beloved person or hatred without such knowledge of the hated person are rather projections of one's own immature character than responses to objective, ascertained qualities. The close relations between feelings and cognitions found in Spinoza an eloquent and convincing exponent. His definition of passions as inadequate ideas reflects, no doubt, an intellectualistic bias. But his brilliant insights into the dynamic relationship between emotions and ideational contents have been verified and validated in contemporary psychological and psychiatric studies.

Adjustment to various environments is not an automatic process. Between a stimulus and a response there are mediating psychological functions in the form of perceptions, emotions, and thoughts. None of these copies or mirrors a value-neutral reality. The perceived, understood, and felt object or event is a small segment of reality, selected and interpreted in the light of physiological and social exigencies. Feelings play an important role in this selective process. They direct our consciousness to objects and qualities which may further or hamper self-preservation and self-enhancement. Perceptions and cognitions tell us what a given object is in its essential properties, feelings inform us about their efficacies from the point of view of our weal and woe. The adaptive or adjustive value of mild feelings is very great. It rests on their correlation with perceptive and cognitive data. The fear felt in a threatening situation is invaluable. The same applies to anger and resentment in the face of real obstructions and hostilities. The adjustive value of emotions decreases with their reality-incongruence which is at the root of violent and persevering passions.

Such passions, instead of serving thought, subjugate it; instead of making thought abide by the threatening situation, force it to dwell on imaginary situations. The persistence of strong emotions deprives consciousness of its intentional representative features, the most essential elements in our rational moral conduct.

CHAPTER IV

THE PLACE OF REASON IN CONDUCT

Man's happiness and misery, joys and sorrows, hopes and despairs, aspirations and frustrations are the raw materials out of which a rational ethics tries to obtain a moral order of social harmony. The fact that feelings are the primordial data of morals does not preclude an objective ethics.[1] What is of decisive importance are the common features of man's sentient nature. If our joys and sorrows differed in kind and were exclusively socially determined, no ethical theory could project a moral order commendable to reason and experience. We are accustomed to speak of a moral order as something which ought to be and thus focus our attention on its aspirational elements. But aspirations must have a basis in actualities in order to function as motivating forces. We can make our desires and feelings more compatible and harmonious, but they must already be compatible in order to become more compatible, they must harmonize in order to become more harmonious. Men respond with similar emotions to certain situations. The loss of a beloved one brings sorrow, no matter where we live and to what culture or society we may belong. Men enjoy good health regardless of their social conditioning. Oppression calls for hatred and resentment which transcend social and national boundaries. Friendliness and kindness are everywhere appreciated. The similarity of emotional responses does not preclude occasional exceptions. We have such exceptions in the perceptive field.

In ethics we often go after the impossible. We are not satisfied with the emotional congruity of the vast majority of people, and view exceptions as valid arguments for subjectivism. We hardly do it in physics, the most exact science. Our physical constructs are predicated on sense data of normally functioning senses. Hallucinations due to impaired senses or mental disfunctions do not discredit an objective physics. Neither should emotional deviations discredit ethics. Psychiatric studies enlighten us as to normal and abnormal emotional reactions, which distinction rests with the shareability of the first and privacy of the latter. Shareability of emotions is predicated on their concatenation with perceptive and cognitive elements.

Feelings wholly uncomparable would not make for social harmony as a fact. Feelings wholly unalterable would not make for social harmony as an ideal. Ideals not suggested by facts are products of fancy, aspirations out of real context. Facts without ideals are dull, devoid of their potential meanings. Any given satisfaction and fulfillment calls for a more enduring satisfaction and fulfillment. In our socialization of desires and interests we always find room for improvement. In doing so we are helped by reason which locates the source of satisfaction and points to a more consummate gratification. Such a reason conceives the ideal as the better, as an ought which stems from the many ascertained facts. By neglecting the latter, reason turns into a spurious guide. Facts most amenable to reason are facts studied, inquired into, not facts ignored or disguised.

Reason is neither a slave nor a master of our impulses and passions. Impulses, desires, emotions, and cognitions have no independent status. They are interdependent elements of the continuum which comprises our psychic life. For the sake of a better understanding we isolate parts of this continuum and thus arrive at discrete phenomena such as perceptions, conations, emotions, and cognitions. Whenever we mistake these discrete abstract entities for real discrete entities, we fall in with the belief in the many "either or" conceptual bifurcations in the form of emotivism, rationalism, voluntarism, sensualism, and what not. The facts appealed to by each exclusive "ism" are more apparent than real, for the facts appealed to are taken out from their wider context. A will which functions separately from feelings and cognitions is nonexistent. Neither is there an intellect detached from impulses, emotions, and desires. In a normal individual there is no primacy of reason or emotion in conduct.

On the conscious level emotions and desires are fused with perceptions and cognitions. The conscious feeling or the conscious desire is the informed feeling or informed desire. Reason enlightens both of them as to their causative factors and the real significance of objects and events. Desire and emotion tend to impute value, reason looks for its objective constituents; desire and emotion urge for immediate response, reason delays the latter by bringing to a better awareness the possible consequences of an act. By the way of an imaginative projection the contemplated act is adjudicated in its fittingness to the given situation, and in its widest bearing on our own as well as the well-being of other people. Desire strives for satisfaction, emotion intensifies this drive. Reason reflects on the ends of desire, their feasibility and appropriateness in the light of personal and social integration. The function of reason is "to clarify and define the ends of endeavor and to relate them to one another, to disclose the nature of the forces, internal and external, necessary for their realization, to insist on the widest consideration of all the claims, that are relevant and the greatest impartiality in dealing with them, and, in cases of conflict whether within the individual or between the individuals, to avoid the use of repression or force and to seek rather than to evoke willing acceptance. Desires or preferences so informed or guided would be rational desires or preferences."²

A critical appraisal of the place of reason in conduct does not square with the widespread trends of intellectualism and emotivism. The first assigns to reason the motivating power of action, the latter ascribes it to emotions. Neither reason nor emotion motivates conduct. Impulses and desires do it. Reason directs or redirects them, emotion reinforces or obstructs them. Pleasure and displeasure are results and not causes of acting. Ethical hedonism (subjective as well as social) interprets pleasures as motives and objectives of conduct. In reality we are motivated by ends we try to implement, the bio-chemical imbalance we seek to restore, by felt obstacles we endeavor to remove, and the many tensions we would like to reduce.

Rationalism has been the prevailing moral philosophy since Socrates. The appeal it still enjoys rests less with its true and valid assertions than with its comforting view. There is no need for a patient observation of facts in solving moral problems. The right and wrong are out there to be grasped by reason, which intuits them apart from the actualities of social life. This rationalism has brought about a sound reaction on the part of those thinkers who have been less biased against the conative and emotive nature of man. But they have moved to another extreme not less untenable than rationalism—to ethical emotivism. By concentrating exclusively on the impulses, desires, and emotions they fail to understand the proper role of practical reason which narrows the gap between impulses and desires, and emotions and cognitions. Practical reason does not decree a priori norms of conduct any more than theoretical reason decrees such laws for nature. It discovers norms of conduct in the give and take, harmony and discord, cooperation and aggression entailed by living together.

The function of reason in moral conduct is manifold.

Reason enlightens us as to intrinsic ends and extrinsic means; it helps us to distinguish between genuine and spurious goods; it makes us avail ourselves of our own cumulative experiences as well as those of other people in reconciling conflicts; it lends foresight to our desires and passions; it operates in the organization of desires by a consistent articulation and impartial appraisal of them in the light of social requirements. "In trying to see how reason works here and what the differences are between action that, in a moral sense, is right and reasonable and that which is arbitrary and unjust, we shall (fortunately) need no special powers of insight or appreciation vouchsafed only to the elect. Nothing more is needed than reliable knowledge and good will in the understanding and evaluation of matters of public knowledge and issues of common concern. Nothing less, however, will suffice."[3] The goods and evils rest with our sentient nature and the objective efficacies of objects and events. No reasoning can remake an unsatisfaction into a satisfaction, a frustration into a fulfillment, an obstacle of growth into an implement of growth. But reason helps our sentient nature to discern the fleeting, transitory goods and the genuine, enduring, time-tested goods, the spurious and genuine values. Reason transforms our impulsive behavior into a principled conduct. In justifying conduct from a moral point of view reason appeals to factual evidence and the implicit valuational norms centering on the common good, as a heuristic principle in the process of harmonizing our genuine wants, goals, and aspirations. "Action that combines good judgment and good will in responsibly shared work for a shareable good comes near enough, for our purposes, to a definition of what we mean by conduct that meets the requirements of rational morality."[4]

There is little disagreement about ultimate ends of the good life. To live is to strive for self-preservation, for a life above the mere subsistence level, for a life free from drudgery, want, and fear, for a life of abundance, of security, affection, and belonging. Reason can neither justify nor deny these intrinsic values which have their roots in our sentient nature. Man's bio-psychological and social nature is such that these ends appear desirable. Whenever we question these intrinsic values we reveal some lack of vitality, despair of attaining them, or callousness to our fellow men to whom we deny basic values and rights. The validation of intrinsic values is not the proper domain of reason. Reason in conjunction with experience is supreme as to the best means and alternative courses of action in implementing ultimate ends. Those who challenge fundamental values and rights of other people never question their own rights. Since the challenge of other people's values is in itself irrational, no rational argument will prevail. The full fledged egoist or a self-centered tribalistic group is subject for moral training, and not a subject for an ethical discourse. Both lack the fundamental requirements of such discourse: adherence to empirical evidence and reasonableness which calls for consistency and valid rules of thinking.

CHAPTER V

FREEDOM AND LICENSE

Human behavior is always motivated. Being motivated means to have a causal determinant. Because our behavior is causally determined, we can study it scientifically, that is, we are able to arrive at true generalizations and predictions. The lasting contributions of Freud are his invaluable insights into the causal nexus of our total psychic life, the conscious as well as the unconscious or subconscious.

The empirical study of human behavior is primarily concerned with its sources and causes. The latter we divide into physiological and social. The first comprise basic biological needs and drives, the second stand for social drives or motives. Physiological and social drives work together. The moment we are born, our biological needs are subject to social determinants such as approval and disapproval, customs of eating and drinking, and the various norms related to the sex drive.

Motives or social drives may be described as socially elaborated needs. Needs are inborn, motives are learned, acquired. While human physiological drives are everywhere the same, motives may differ from nation to nation, from culture to culture. In some self-assertion may be a vital motive, in some it may discouraged; in some the competitive urge may be encouraged, in some discouraged; in some the acquisition of material goods may be overestimated, in some underplayed; gregariousness may be cherished in some, and solitariness in other societies.

Motives or social drives differ from physiological needs in many respects: a physiological need eventuates in a diffuse, a motive in an organized activity; a physiological need calls for an immediate response, a motive works as a prospective end, it makes us look ahead to the possible consequences of an act. Motives may be conscious as purposes or may be subconscious as acquired habits or repressed experiences. No single motive has a corresponding single biological need. Behind a single motive there are various biological needs. Since motives are acquired, their number is very great: the urge for power, prestige, economic gain, self-assertion, respect for others, interest in science, art, religion, cooperation, competition, the urge to conform or reform. The most common motives of a transcultural setting are: the urge for social status and approval, loyalty, intellectual curiosity, artistic expression, religious worship, belonging, affection, companionship, security, and achievement.

Concerning our knowledge of man there is a general agreement that man occupies a unique position. He alone can examine conditions of his life; he alone is able to accumulate wisdom related to his needs and implement it in facing precarious situations; he alone can postpone an immediate response to a given stimulus and use deliberation before embarking upon a certain course of action. While other living creatures can adapt themselves to a given environment, man alone is able to change this environment to fulfill his wants.

Man is intimately connected with the total environment. The exigencies of his existence are contigent upon an orderly and uniform nature, of which he is a part, subject to the same laws. He shares with other living organisms the urge for self-preservation, metabolistic processes, adaptability, and sensitivity. But he differs from them in many aspects. Of these the most important is his almost unlimited ability to learn. Because of this faculty man alone enjoys tradition, the wealth of cumulative meanings and values transmitted from generation to generation, and constantly enriched by new trials, new insights, and new records of successes and failures.

Man is a rational being. Whenever he advances in his struggle for survival, his intellect is the driving agent. Because of his reason and symbolic language man transforms brute facts into abstractions which make for classification, identification and explanation of events. The latter in the form of phenomenal, conscious, cognitive entities endure in our memory and become subject to a lively shift in our imagination. Out of such visionary projections possibilities turn into realities. Man's rational nature strives for that sound balance between tradition and innovation which alone can do full justice to the limitations and opportunities of growth. We are prospective beings able to anticipate the future by virtue of our retrospective faculty for dwelling in the past. A lively communion with the spiritual heritage fosters the sense for the significant. It helps to treasure and augment the realm of values, and thus preserves and promotes cultural continuity.

Not less noble than man's reason is his social and emotive nurtured endowment: sympathy, compassion, love for his fellow men, humility before God, and a deep sense of insignificance in the vast universe. Deprive human nature of these character-building emotions and attitudes, and man's intellect may become a cold-blooded instrument of destruction. The highest moral ideal we cherish today belongs to the religious tradition. It took science more than two thousand years to prove what was a visionary certainty to the few religious saints and prophets, that all races have a common origin, that all men are of the same kind. There is no higher moral principle than that so eloquently expressed by Kant: "Behave so as to use humanity, whether in your own person or in the person of another, always as an end, never as merely a means," and this injunction epitomizes the religious doctrine of the equality and dignity of men.

Knowledge of man's nature is crucial to any elucidation of the vexing problem of freedom which intends to be more than a mere linguistic analysis. The term freedom defies an exact definition. Words elusive of precise definitions are of two kinds: vacuous symbols devoid of any referent, and symbols replete with meaning. Freedom belongs to the latter class. Its all-pervasiveness defies any exact cognitive connotation. This particularity freedom shares with many other basic symbols such as love, hatred, experience, goodness, etc. We learn to use these symbols once we are able to verbalize. We associate them with objects and events which are very close to us, and may employ them correctly although their referents are various and often vague. By enumeration of a number of denotative instances of freedom, its cognitive import becomes clear. Of a sick man whose health is impaired for a considerable time we say that he lacks freedom of movement; if a man acts under external pressure and internal duress, he is not free; a man in prison is deprived of most liberties; natural catastrophes such as drought, flood, famine, cripple man's freedom by reducing the alternative courses of action; bias, ignorance, superstition may transform men into mere automata. Whenever we enjoy health, our movements are free; whenever we find our life protected from aggression, want and fear, we experience freedom. Finding opportunities to implement aims is an instance of enhanced freedom. All these cases prove that freedom is not an abstract entity apart from our activities. Unless we act in one way or another, unless we conceive goals and work toward their fulfillment, we do not experience freedom. Hence we may characterize freedom as a quality of behavior.

The latter may be obstructed or furthered. Conquering of obstacles is one form of freedom, implementing of aims is another form of freedom.

Freedom is a quality of experiences. The latter are of two kinds: experiences we wish to last, and experiences we want to cease or avoid. The consciousness of freedom grows with the first and diminishes with the second. The cheerful, enhanced experiences are conducive to our self-preservation and self-expansion. Thwarting, gloomy occurrences and sad experiences are at the root of disintegration and desocialization. Here freedom is at its minimum.

Freedom is a quality of our aims. Goals may liberate or enslave us, may elevate us to spiritual heights or bring us down to the level of irrational, preying beasts. Aims which widen our mental and moral horizon are freedom-sustaining and freedom-promoting ends; aims which make us act on a mere impulse are freedom-destroying objectives. Tasks which court frustrations cripple our freedom; tasks which add strength to our will-endeavors make for experiences of enhanced freedom.

Freedom is a quality of our character. It connotes the degree of integration, from a personal as well as from a social point of view. Freedom grows with pervasive interests, creative aspirations, and social requirements; it diminishes with isolation, selfishness, and aggressiveness. Freedom is not license. Licentious behavior is uncontrolled, unrestricted behavior which enslaves man in all spheres of action. It confines him to the immediate; it blinds him to the desirability and feasibility of goals; it distorts his sense of reality and sense of values, the most important factors behind a full, happy life. To be free is not to do what we wish to do, but to want things which are necessary to maintain the ever threatened equilibrium. Neither on a mere physiological level, nor on the psychological and social plane of living can we achieve an enduring satisfaction without a steady ordering and organizing of our impulses, desires, and goals. Freedom and order complete each other. Licentious beings are not only immoral in their inconsiderate indulgence in transient and violent desires, but very unhappy creatures unable to submerge in a greater social unit, incapable of widening their interests and goals. If there is anything man values most it is freedom to grow and expand. License cripples self-realization, for it undermines its essential conditions: organization of experiences, directing impulses and passions toward a shareable life predicated on conduct of an enlightened prudence which makes us realize how insignificant and helpless we are in isolation, a prudence which teaches us that our own freedom is contingent upon the freedom of our fellow men with whom we share the same vicissitudes of living, the same joys and sorrows, the same predicament of being thrust into a world full of hopes and despairs, fulfillments and frustrations.

As rational beings we are able to utilize natural and social uniformities for our own self-determination and self-realization. This is the essence of freedom. It consists in making the most of the causal nexus, and not in defying or acting contrary to it. An indeterministic view of nature as well as an uncritical determinism which confuses causality with necessity are not true to fact. Man's behavior is neither a chance phenomenon nor a result of necessary laws beyond his control. No social tendency or institution is inevitable once we realize the conditions which have brought them forth. As in the life of a single individual, so in the existence of a nation there is an amount of unpredictability resulting from free choice. Freedom of choice is not freedom from causality. Choice is a matter of opportunities giving us a wide range of alternative courses of action. Situations propitious to freedom are situations conducive to our wants and aspirations. There is always a factor of human creativity or inventiveness. The latter make for historical unpredictability

—a fact we have no reason to regret. A complete predictable life would be a life devoid of novelty. While we cannot predict human history, we can control it to a certain extent. We can make it into a record of senseless bloody battles or into an inspiring record of cultural growth. Whether we are going to shape it in the first direction or the second depends upon our will and courage to avail ourselves of that knowledge of man which is true to fact, and reject the prevailing myth of man's inherent pugnacity, of a nature opaque to human aspiration—a myth which would like us to believe that social evolution and devolution are part and parcel of a cosmic evolution and devolution where man's decisions count very little.

Freedom of choice is the basis for man as a moral, accountable agent. His voluntary acts differ from mere impulsive and habitual responses in two important aspects. They postpone an immediate reaction to given stimuli and situations, and are directed by ends in view in the form of values, standards, and ideals. Voluntary acts follow deliberation. A free choice is not a whimsical one. It is a choice of the most desirable and effective course. Our moral freedom depends upon many factors: social habits, emotional sensitivity, right foresight, and intelligent planning. The quality of moral choice reflects the kind of personality we have become and the kind of society in which we live. Whenever we talk about freedom we usually stress our privileges and rights and blissfully forget their complementary duties and obligations. We ought to remind ourselves that privileges grow from obligations, that rights come from duties. Genuine freedom requires a fusion of both.

The most basic presupposition of science of nature and science of man is the principle of causality. Whether we study a natural phenomenon or man's behavior, the causal nexus is the guiding norm. Stimuli and responses, deliberation, execution of acts, and thinking in general exhibit uniformities which make for ascertained knowledge. At a time when man looked upon nature in terms of magic or fate or hidden purposes, he indulged in fanciful outlooks, devoid of any proper understanding and control of nature.

The belief in causality is known as determinism. A denial of causality goes under the name of indeterminism. The futile controversy between the advocates of the two contradictory beliefs, especially with regard to man's will, is based on a misconception of the nature of causality. Causality, as Hume so eloquently and convincingly pointed out, stands for a constant recurring conjunction between two events, and not for necessity in the sense of a must or inevitable force or tie which obtains between them. Between man's motives and actions, between his stimuli and responses, between his upbringing and reactions there is a uniform connection, but not a necessary bond which would, indeed, deprive him of any liberty to think, to express, and to act. Where man lacks such a liberty, causality is not the underlying reason. The underlying reasons are manifold: physical or psychological restraint or compulsion, frustrations of basic and acquired needs, ignorance, and the absence of alternative courses of action. Physical, psychological, and social pressures may be of such grave nature that no deliberation could ensue. When such pressures are discernible, man ceases to be accountable for his behavior. But whenever they are absent, we do make him accountable in spite of the fact that his actions are causally determined. Given no causal regularities, our freedom would be illusory. Our control of nature and our social interaction are predicated on a uniform sequence of events. Education itself is predicated on causal uniformities. It presupposes that ideas and ideals will affect behavior, and certain motives and emotions will prevail. Moral responsibility requires a will acting in conformity with certain motives, certainly not a will free from antecedent causal determinants. Causality and moral responsibility go together just as a uniform nature and man's capacity to control it complete each other. Man is both an object of causality and subject of freedom. Our uniform behavior enhances the freedom of our fellow man with whom we interact, and the uniform behavior of our fellow men increases our own freedom.

CHAPTER VI

ON HAPPINESS
(Eudaemonia)

Most common and most pervasive ideas are difficult to define. Happiness is one of these cognitively elusive concepts. The nearest verbalization would be an exalted feeling of bodily and mental satisfaction. The sentiment which stands for happiness is an intense, enduring, and fructifying emotion of well-being. Since human existence entails many frustrations, an attitude of indifference and renunciation is praised as most suitable to happiness. By doing it, we fail to realize that with each renunciation we cultivate an emotional insensitivity to the unpleasant as well as pleasant features of life. To live fully is to interact with the various environments. Happiness, as Aristotle correctly saw, is the reward of a very active life whose consummatory effect it epitomizes. It is not indifference to or willful rationalization of an obstacle or frustration which makes for genuine satisfaction, but rather a realistic appraisal of it, and an intelligent, concentrated effort to remedy it. It is not an extirpation of vital impulses and passions men cherish as a desirable end, although their socially conditioned self or conscience may conform to an ideology which extols such an ideal. But behind this negative ideal there are frustrated needs, wishes, and aspirations which affirm the good of wordly joys.

"Man is an acting being. Pleasantness and unpleasantness

are epiphenomena and not motives of psychic functions. There is no other reason for acting, discharging of energies, than growth and expansion. We do not act because of pleasure, rather because we act, we experience pleasure and displeasure. Hedonism converts these contingent, emotional occurrences, which are results or effects, into causes. It fails entirely to describe and explain our volitions,"[1] which go after objects worthy of pursuit.

"True happiness comes from our enhanced spiritual activities. Knowledge is a vigorous solace only for those who take in their stride the pangs and discomforts which true, unbiased thinking entails. The bliss that follows fairness and kindness toward mankind springs from our sympathy for our fellow men. How could we ever enjoy a generous deed if this deed were not the result of a struggle, of obstacles which had been overcome? No great work of art falls into the lap of its creator without the many hardships and renunciations that creation exacts. If we desire to share his enjoyments, we must encompass all his life which finds expression in his work. When we read about a great deed of a man, we derive pleasure from it to the extent that we are able to live through all the events which brought it about. If we want to know the bliss of love, we must accept its tragic vicissitudes. We do not grow and expand by pleasures, but by activities which invoke pleasures."[2]

To live a happy life we must cultivate our impulses, passions, conations and cognitions in their constant interaction with the physical and social environment. Self-realization is too precarious to exclude defeat. To live a full life we must risk failures. If we make ourselves immune to the many perplexing and unpleasant situations, our happiness is bound to become spurious. Peace of mind or soul is not won by comforting contemplations that evil is not real, or by a self-enclosed consciousness which takes flights into fancy. The true peace of mind is won by a successful struggle with the precarious elements of the physical and social world we are thrust into. Immunity to the reality of evil is immunity to the reality of good, immunity to sorrow is immunity to joy. The opposite of happiness is not sadness or a painless state, but rather depression which is "the inability to feel . . . to experience joy, as well as the inability to experience sadness." [3]

Although opinions differ as to what constitutes happiness, certain conditions are accepted as essential for its occurrence. Health is probably the most basic factor. Physical and mental health are both a personal and social achievement. Individual efforts toward good health are of little avail if one happens to live in a social environment where magic and superstitions reign in matters of health. Like physical health, so, too, mental health transcends particular social idiosyncrasies. Its essential features are: integration, organization, and social relatedness. We are mentally sound if we are able to order the inchoate elements of our experiences, to integrate impulses and desires, and construct an outlook on nature and society in accordance with the principle of reality.

Social relatedness or emergence, the ability to accept and give affection is an invaluable source of happiness.[4] Living in a world of uncertainty and precariousness, we must emerge into a wider unit in order to escape the morbid thought of a narrow self-enclosed consciousness. Social relatedness counteracts the feeling of forlornness and anxiety by engendering and promoting creative interests which alone give meaning to life. A constructive social relatedness feeds most gratifying feelings of love and sympathy which lead to both an affirmation of life and a deep reverence for life.

An animal may be satisfied and content with food and shelter. Not so man. Studies in neuroses and psychoses, juvenile delinquency and adult crimes, show that frustration of psychic and social needs is as harmful as deprivation of bodily needs. Man strives for affection, for belonging, for freedom and status, which needs enhance a salutary self-respect and respect for others.

The key-words for happiness are balance, harmony, and integration. Good physical health rests within an harmonious fulfillment of all organic drives. Good mental health is predicated on an integration of drives and motives, impulses, desires, emotions and cognitions. True happiness comes from a concourse of needs and their fulfillment in the form of values.

A satisfactory ethics of human relations will take care that the essentials of the moral life square with essentials of the good life. Such an ethics will reject both the belief that the moral good or the good of all is a mere summation of individual goods, and the belief that there is a sharp dichotomy between the happiness of each single person and the social, common good. There is neither such a harmony nor such an antithesis between these two.

Reflecting upon man's social nature, upon the undeniable fact that social isolation is the severest punishment we can mete out to a criminal, we must wonder about the disheartening failure of better social relations. Could it be (as modern psychiatry suggests) that man's aggressions have been adjustive techniques to ward off the many tensions and frustrations society has in store for him? Could it be that man inflicts misery and injury on his fellow man because tribal moral practices and codes deprive him of the essentials of the good life? Could it be that the injunction "love your neighbor" fails to include the very person to whom it is addressed? We do not know whether all aggressions are results of accumulated frustrations. But certainly many stem from them.

A rational ethics with a universal appeal will be eudaemonistic but not hedonistic, for it will not mistake pleasure for a constituent of the good life instead of a concomitant. It will be idealistic by following the heuristic principle of the common good without neglecting each person's genuine good. "Undoubtedly we should desire the happiness of those whom we love, but not as an alternative to our own. In fact, the whole antithesis between the self and the rest of the world, which is implied in the doctrine of self-denial, disappears as soon as we have any genuine interests in persons and things outside ourselves."[5]

CHAPTER VII.

FACTS AND VALUES
FACTUAL AND VALUE JUDGMENTS

Only sentient beings, endowed with capacities for desire and aversion, pleasure and pain, fulfillment and frustration, experience values and disvalues—things and events we call good and bad, beautiful and ugly, worthy or unworthy of being preserved and augmented or discarded. Preferential behavior is deeply rooted in every living creature. But only in man do instinctive value responses become cognitively cumulative, enriched by our own experiences as well as by experiences of other people. Without a cultivated sense of values and disvalues man could not survive, still less enhance his life. Survival on a mere physiological plane is predicated upon a proper grasp of objects which answer to our basic needs. Our enhanced life depends upon tested appraisals of objects which minister to our higher psychological and social drives, such as affection, freedom, security, belonging, self-esteem and regard for others. Our sentient nature registers events as pleasing and unpleasing, agreeable or disagreeable, gratifying or frustrating. Our cognitive nature looks for objective constituents of values and disvalues. Of the innumerable qualities of objects, we are primarily interested in the actual and potential efficacies related to our needs, basic and derivative. In all probability, our intellectual curiosity, the urge to know, to explore and manipulate objects stems from our valuational nature. The pleasing and displeasing, the liked and disliked events call for knowledge as an instrument of prediction and control. Knowledge of the structure and interconnections of events is intimately fused with our preferential behavior, rooted in the desire to preserve the good things in life and eradicate the evil things.

In order to know what is conducive to survival, to discover objects which satisfy our wants, please our senses, elevate our emotions and conations, we must know the structure and causal nexus of events. Factual judgments describe the latter. Value judgments are concerned with "how well a thing can minister to our wants, desires, aims, needs, aspirations, ideals, and the like."[1]

Value judgments add a great deal to our factual judgments. They tell us what objects and events do to our bio-social nature. To assume that values are nothing else than mere emotive responses to value-neutral events is to disregard the blatant fact that our feelings, drives, and goals are "enmeshed in the contexts of things and events."[2]

The widespread division of the realm of facts and the realm of value is based on many untenable assumptions. Here are just a few of the current beliefs: that man has a disinterested curiosity to know nature; that whenever human wants and goals enter a scientific inquiry, the result of the investigation must of necessity be a distorted picture of reality; that the incredible advance of natural sciences is primarily due to the fact that our likings and dislikings have been completely eliminated, and preferences discarded; that values are subjective responses which elude any scientific approach; and that it is meaningless to talk about values apart from our appreciation, for the latter constitutes their sole meaning. A disinterested curiosity is a semantic confusion. "No curiosity, no urge to know is devoid of some want or interest. Because man has the goal of improving his struggle for the necessities of living he arrives at knowledge of nature. Human desires, likes, and aims are at the root of scientific discoveries. That many discoveries have no immediate practical pertinence does not invalidate the statement that only interest-having creatures embark upon the road to knowledge, for the interest in social prestige and recognition is as vital as the need for food, shelter, and clothing." [3]

Facts are alluring or disappointing, pleasant or unpleasant, furthering or frustrating, and our value terms denote and connote these qualities. The subjectivistic theories of value which interpret values as sentiments or emotions or socially conditioned responses which make us impute worth to things, are not true to fact. The good things and evil things in life, health and sickness, joys and pains, gratifications and frustrations, abundance and deprivation are not mere feelings or opinions. No opinion can transform suffering into gratification, no social convention can make a frustration into a fulfillment, no idiosyncrasy can change an obstacle of growth into an increment. "In order to treasure the good things in life man has been given many assets, among them the most important is the gift of perceiving, retaining, augmenting and transmitting. Emotion reinforces the memory of valuable events. Value is felt because of the memory of its conducive effects. Feelings are basic indicators of reality. In conjunction with our memory, perceptive and cognitive abilities they are an invaluable asset." [4] Detached from the latter they may become a great liability so acute in neurotic and psychotic patients.

Values and disvalues although rooted in facts are not identical with facts. They are objects and events appraised in relation to our wants, aims and aspirations, as gratifying or frustrating, as experiences we would like to endure or experiences we would like to see come to an end. The separation of facts and values is one of the most flabbergasting artifacts which has brought about endless futile discussions, suggestions and countersuggestions. Values and disvalues are experienced in concatenation with facts. Whether we call an object beautiful or ugly, behavior good or bad, there is always a state of affairs to which we apply these value terms. The fusion of facts and values is a persisting trait of human existence. To live is to choose, to select. No object or event is acted upon as a value-free stimulus, rather as an object or event pregnant with valuational meanings. In the presence of an object there is our past appreciation of the object, our fulfilled or frustrated expectations, our fund of knowledge, our beliefs and attitudes, shaped by, and shaping, the explicit or implicit selective norm or standard which directs us in our search for the actual and potential properties of an object or event from the point of view of our well-being. The norm or standard of valuation is an outgrowth of experience. The good which figures as a selective and prescriptive norm in our conduct is the good previously experienced, the good remembered, registered from the standpoint of gratification. Any new fulfillment strengthens the standard, any frustration calls for its modification.

"Value terms are standards and results of appraisal. This twofold role, the intimate fusion of descriptive and prescriptive properties of value concepts, has been a subject of endless controversies. Much quibbling can be avoided if we concentrate on the cumulative role of our experiences. If we could approach an immediate situation psychologically and sociologically in a pristine way, the first experience would become a standard for the second, the second for the third, and so forth. Such a state of affairs would deprive us of learning from other generations and other periods by way of the actual cultural heritage." [5] The latter "transforms the vast repository of values into a continuous, living experience where principles or standards of conduct are operative on different levels, either as unreflective customary norms, or as reflective principles open to novel situations and corrigible by new experiments in living together." [6]

Value terms are also results of appraisals. Whenever we predicate the terms good and bad of objects and events, we do so after a series of descriptive statements recording observable properties. The cognitive meaning is identical with these verifiable properties. The prescriptive meaning indicates and validates the empirically verified behavior in the light of a standard. The norm of the good or right tells us "whether the adjudicated person adhered to, or violated the explicit or tacit moral covenant upon which every community, even the most primitive, is founded. By moral approving and disapproving we do more than express our likes or dislikes, our admiration or contempt. We make objective claims of an impartial valuation. We record our experiences and predict similar experience on the part of other people." [7]

Since man relates himself to his fellow men in various ways according to his dispositions, his knowledge of social exigencies, and given situations, no society could survive without objective norms of behavior, enforced or agreed upon voluntarily. To place the moral good in emotions would jeopardize social relations. Not better is any theory of the moral life which centers on desires and interests of single individuals. The morally good life is an harmonious integration of individual goods. The standard of the moral life consists of principles which balance inhibitions and exhibitions, guide our deliberations on the plane of imaginary projections of contemplated actions. These principles have the nature of commands for people with a minimum of moral conscience and consciousness, poor sensitivity to social requiredness, and underdeveloped intellectual faculties. For mature (socially, emotionally, and intellectually) people moral norms are autonomous rules, based on mutual trust and respect, freely assented to. On the higher level of sociability norms of conduct become interiorized.

The problem of values is baffling if we try to solve what we do not understand. If we look for values as immutable essences, permeating the world and waiting for our intuitive or contemplative grasp, we are groping in darkness. "There was a time when man indulged in similar speculations about nature. He searched for the essence of all events, for the everlasting in the flux of things, and as long as he wasted his energies on grasping some eternal truth, his results were very poor. It was Pythagoras, one of the greatest thinkers before Plato, who realized the importance of numbers as expressive means for the relations of events. Well, we today do not ponder any more upon his speculations on numbers. We rather dismiss them as such. But about the eminence of Pythagoras' discovery that to know things means to comprehend their standing in relation to other things, to follow up their transitions, there cannot be disagreement. Science began to develop with this discovery." [8]

Whatever we know of an event it is its interconnection with other events, the ways it relates itself to other events. What applies to natural phenomena, the spatio-temporal events, holds equally true of psychic and social phenomena. What do we know about mind, reason, character, desires, and emotions? We do not know them as entities or substantive essences. We know them as functional phenomena as they relate themselves to other phenomena. We lay hold of them as causes and effects, antecedents and consequences.

Unprejudiced inquiries into facts have led to the dynamic world-outlook. Instead of speculating about essences or intrinsic qualities of things man began to concentrate on what a given object does, how it generates and what it brings forth. Once we shift our question "what is an object or event?" to the question "how does an object or event occur?" we find ourselves embarked upon the process of ascertaining and augmenting warranted knowledge. With values the procedures cannot be different if we forsake fruitless quibblings for a reliable knowledge.

Our value terms describe events from certain perspectives.

The fact that the same event may be expressed by a factual or valuative judgment (e.g., X inflicted pain on Y, X is bad) shows how intimately connected they are.[9] "The subject-object relation, which is characteristic of all our knowledge of events, becomes more apparent in value judgments. The valued object and valuing subject are complementary units. The efficacies of objects are determined by our own responses. To assume that values are nothing but psychic effects is to believe in responses without external stimuli. Our gratifications are not random experiences. They have causes and effects. They come from objects and are directed toward objects. Things and events must have certain properties, potentialities, in order to become objects of desires, emotions, and evaluative thought."[10]

"The concept of value permeates our life at every step. We prefer one thing to another, we shift attention from one event to another, praise one behavior and condemn another, we like and dislike, and whenever we do so, we value. Behind our passions, interests, willed actions is the belief that they are worth-while. We attach to them different degrees of importance or value. We speak of good and bad aims, noble and mean actions, beautiful and ugly objects, pious and impious intentions and deeds. Our whole life moves between attraction and repulsion. Events are alluring, enhancing, fascinating or repugnant, loathsome, obnoxious. In fact, we not only value, but are always aware of a scale of values."[11] Their ranking of high and low, wide and narrow, deep or shallow is a function of both the degree of gratification on the part of the subject and the various efficacies on the part of the object. Value comprises both.

There is a widespread agreement that we ascribe values to whatever gives satisfaction, and disvalue to whatever causes dissatisfaction. But the status of values and disvalues has been a subject of lasting controversy. For some thinkers, values and disvalues are our inner states of mind, our feelings, desires and interests; for other philosophers, values and disvalues have an independent ontological existence. These two schools of thought, although widespread and endlessly debated, have no basis in facts. The available knowledge related to our valuational, preferential behavior refutes the bifurcation of facts and values, common to all kinds of value subjectivism and metaphysical value realism. The subjectivistic theories neglect to investigate the sources of agreeable and disagreeable feelings, the roots of our desires and interests; the metaphysical interpretation detaches the origin and function of values from their complementary unit—the sentient human being. The first school denies to value judgments the status of cognition; the second makes its cognitive import contingent upon a mysterious intuition, an exclusive gift of a few individuals.

The value realism, set forth by Plato, and revived by Scheler and Hartmann, has no basis in ascertained facts. No matter what value we reflect upon, it is a state of affairs which we adjudicate in value terms, good, bad, better, worse, etc. What beauty or goodness is supposed to be apart from beautiful or good things, apart from the effects they have on us, is incomprehensible. Value terms do not tell us about values as isolated, non-spatial or nontemporal entities or essences. They refer to specific states of affairs as they affect us, as they answer to our wants and aspirations. Behind value realism, predicated on the assumption of existing immutable, perfect entities, independent of the flux of events and human consciousness, is our propensity to project as real what we wish and desire. The brute facts of existence excite our imagination more than our creative intelligence and courage. Instead of implementing what we aspire to, we picture it fulfilled and dwell in images which are congenial to our wishes. For lack of an intelligent encounter with real perplexities, we rationalize, cover up, find all kinds of palliatives to render the situation more in accord with our own desires. Instead of reshaping reality in the light of its efficacies, we are satisfied with mere imaginative projections. "By reading the characteristic feature of any man's castles in the air you can make a shrewd guess as to his underlying desires which are frustrated. What is difficulty and disappointment in real life becomes conspicuous achievement and triumph in revery; what is negative in fact will be positive in the image drawn by fancy; what is vexation in conduct will be compensated for in high relief in idealizing imagination." [12]

Not less untenable than value realism is value subjectivism which identifies values and disvalues with our sentiments of liking and disliking. Our feelings, desires, and interests not only are important factors in our value and disvalue experience (which is obvious) but they are supposed to be their sole constituent factors. Values, no doubt, are bound up with our sentient and conative nature, with our feelings, desires, and interests. But this fact proves as little the subjective status of values as the fact of our perceptive and cognitive consciousness would prove an epistemological subjectivism, predicated on the assumption that our perceptions and cognitions are the sole determinants of reality. What feelings, desires, and interests are in respect to values, sensations are in regard to objects and events. They are the raw material out of which we arrive at the vital distinction between the real and the apparent, between an objective and a mere subjective world, between objective and mere subjective, imputed values. The genuine real is related to our perceptive and cognitive faculties in its being understood, not in its independent existence. The genuine values are related to our sentient nature in their being appreciated, not in their objective efficacies. To believe that feeling and desiring constitute the valuable is as naive and harmful as the belief that perceiving and cognizing constitute the real. In matters of fact and values we are under the impact of external objects, events, and situations which give rise to our experiences.

Although value judgments show a greater variance than judgments of facts, common to both is the intentional reference. By designating an act or a person good, we do more than evince our feelings of liking or approval. We claim a correspondence of our preference with objectively ascertained qualities of the appreciated object. The argumentative character of value judgments, the distinction between rational and irrational valuations, cultivated and uncultivated taste, are predicated on the assumption that there is something in the object or event which lends our value judgments some degree of objectivity. What guarantees the latter is the fact that we share our value experiences with other thinking beings.

We hardly question objective constituents of values concerning things which satisfy our physiological needs. With the advance of biochemistry we learn that at the root of our physiological preferences there are distinctive qualities of objects which call for felt satisfactions. Even in such elusive values as beauty and ugliness we recognize the validity of different degrees of aesthetic appreciation, a distinction which would be meaningless if not for the accompanying belief that there is something in the artistic object itself which calls for the appreciation. As to moral approval and disapproval, we certainly do not live up to the tenets of value subjectivism. We recognize intelligent and unintelligent, genuine and spurious or mere imitative approvals.

The customary distinction between the desired and the desirable, the approved and worthy of being approved or approvable, loved and lovable points to two senses of values, subjective and objective. The fact that something is liked or desired is an unreflected datum of valuation, the likable or desirable is the appraised object of valuation. The latter implies that the liked or desired object meets certain conditions. "It is, in effect, a judgment that the thing "will do." It involves a prediction; it contemplates a future in which the thing will continue to serve; it will do. It asserts a consequence the thing will actively institute; it will do." [13]

Our value judgments may be immediate, unreflective responses or reflective appraisals of a nurtured taste, "the outcome of experience brought cumulatively to bear on the intelligent appreciation of the real worth of likings and enjoyments. . . . The formation of a cultivated and effectively operative good judgment or taste with respect to what is esthetically admirable, intellectually acceptable and morally approvable is the supreme task set to human beings by the incidents of experience." [14]

The desirable is both the result of an appraisal and the regulatory standard of appraising. Its effectiveness as an evaluating norm depends upon its cognitive import, upon its being grounded in the ascertained facts of social accord and discord. Enjoyments which issue from conduct principled by such effective norms are seldom repented. The latter will always be of a hypothetical nature, subject to modification in accord with the growth of knowledge in general and ever changing social conditions.

"A moral law, like a law in physics, is not something to swear by and stick to at all hazards; it is a formula of the way to respond when specified conditions present themselves. Its soundness and pertinence are tested by what happens when it is acted upon." [15]

The data of ethics are not sense data. To look upon good and bad, right and wrong as intuitively grasped properties or some transcendent essences is to court justified criticism. Feelings, desires, interests, goals and aspirations are at the root of our moral discourse. The good we approve is the liked, desired, the bad we disapprove is the disliked, repelled. But our likes and dislikes, desires and aversions are not detached from their wider environmental context, from the many discernible facts, antecedents and consequences of a predictive reliability. In adjudicating an act as good or bad, right or wrong, we are not referring to our feelings and volitions, but to objective, ascertainable facts. We refer to the beneficial or harmful effects, to the kind of person behind the act, to his cooperative or aggressive traits. All these statements can be tested. Good and bad, right and wrong are persistent elements of our moral consciousness. They epitomize, describe and prescribe certain states of affairs. It is our total experience, the result of social interaction, give and take, claims and counterclaims, precedent and novelty, which are the source of a binding standard. Its satisfactory, consumatory effect is the best guarantee against moral contraventions.

CHAPTER VIII

GOOD AND BAD. RIGHT AND WRONG

Precision of thought and clarity of language are essential requirements of any successful communication. No wonder that many contemporary philosophers are preoccupied with semantic and logical analyses of ethical terms and judgments.[1] But the zest for logical vigor and lucidity of language has blinded them to the intricate elements of our moral experience. The need for ethics stems not so much from the fact that our moral language is vague as from the fact that our desires, aims, and interests conflict. What calls for ethical reflections are "man's incomplete gregariousness,"[2] the frequent disharmony between his emotions and reason, the social sanction of ethical injunctions which have lost their usefulness, and the human proneness to wilfully arbitrate matters of right and wrong. If our moral perplexities were a mere subject of precise definitions, logic would make ethics superfluous. To indulge in such comforting belief is to forget that linguistic and logical confusions are more often effects than causes of moral disagreements. Questions of form do not settle lively issues. Their proper place is not the beginning of an inquiry, but its goal. The success and failure of logical scrutinies in ethics depend on whether or not a clarification of fundamental concepts has its foundation in a warranted knowledge related to man's mainsprings of action, and the opportunities and obstacles of social cohesion.

Clarity of language reflects the degree of exactness of a

given study. Our moral language is vague because our knowledge of man is still full of conjectures and hasty generalizations. Hence, in addition to semantic and logical analyses, ethicists must dwell upon the various social studies in order to disentangle theories from doctrines, ascertained generalizations from mere guesses, and by doing it, integrate the many fragments of informative and explanatory nature into a coherent picture of man's bio-social nature as it is being shaped by, and shapes the various environments. In conjunction with this integrative role logical skill is an asset. Detached from it, the passion for logical vigor makes us embark upon spurious adventures of stipulating and postulating ethical or meta-ethical terms out of context with reality. Only in a constant checking and rechecking against the background of facts can language reveal the structure and connection of events, physical as well as moral. An adequate conceptual framework is predicated on a patient observation of facts.

Our moral language is beset with greater difficulties than our physical language. Very often it is used to conceal and not to express our true desires and values. Its manifold functions—emotive, evocative, ceremonial, and informative—are entangled in one composite whole whose intricacy itself is highly suggestive of simplified schemata. For one thinker the emotive function becomes the exclusive one, for another the evocative or ceremonial or the informative. In addition, our moral language is full of rationalizations. The innumerable social pressures make our verbalization a very poor indicator of what we actually value and disvalue. What appears to semanticists as a moral disagreement may in reality be an agreement if we concentrate on man's total conduct. Our verbalization and sophisticated articulation of our likes and dislikes, approvals and disapprovals are to a high extent motivated by fear of disfavor on the part of society in which we live. Not so our behavior, our tacit and repressed desires, aims and aspirations. They disclose the favorite proverb that in matters of value "meat for one is poison for another" as a travesty of facts. The good things in life are common to man no matter in which culture he lives. The assertion that nothing is good or bad, right or wrong, unless feeling or thinking makes it so, is a dogma of subjectivistic doctrines of values which accentuate the appreciative subject at the expense of the appreciated object and event. Good and bad are discernible elements of the real world. We experience them as opportunities or obstructions which make for gratifications or frustration. "Very many things we simply find to be good or bad; and this direct experience is the basic fact to which all judgments of value are ultimately reducible." [3] We respond with desire to good things and with aversion to bad things not as states of mind, but as events having certain antecedents and consequences, certain properties which may be conducive or detrimental to our well-being.

Even the most primitive human group could not live up to a value subjectivism. Living together is predicated on a consensus as to basic values, on claims and counterclaims, demands and counterdemands concerning rights and their contraventions. No man is a subjectivist when it comes to his own needs and interests. But many people rationalize their callousness to other people's needs and rights as value subjectivism. When their behavior is adjudicated in moral terms, they may dismiss such judgments as mere emotive reactions, devoid of any meaning. Not so when they themselves appraise other people's conduct. Here their judgments make objective claims by appealing to ascertained facts of a social requiredness.

The formation of reliable judgments as to objective constituents of the real and valuable is not an option. It is a vital necessity. Desiring, liking, and striving for objects without knowledge of their verified and verifiable efficacies are the chief factors behind valuational disagreement, not an intractable nature of values themselves. Our tested value experiences make objective claims which can be checked by their predictive expectations upon which we act.

Our moral approvals and disapprovals which appraise given states of affairs in the light of the all-inclusive standard of the well-being of man reveal at the same time the kind of personality we have become—our narrow or wise interests, our emotional maturity or immaturity, our proneness to rationalization and projection, or our objective ratiocination, our moral parochialism or universalism. Serious ethical disagreements are rare among people in whom reflective morality takes the place of an uncritical acceptance of customs and whose attitudes and sentiments are corrigible in the light of new facts. Ethical subjectivism and relativism are contradicted by the universal moral code of great religious prophets of all lands, by great men in art and science, and the untold number of plain people from all walks of life and from every culture, people who have understanding of, and are sensitive to man's needs, and resent with words and deeds the cruelties men mete out to men.

Ethical terms stand for social behavior. Men relate themselves in different ways. They are friendly or hostile, helpful or obstructive, cooperative or aggressive. No matter how ambiguous moral notions may be, good and right are descriptive and prescriptive terms of cooperative responses, bad and wrong are descriptive and prescriptive terms of aggressive actions. Although these two pairs of concepts are closely related—good and bad, right and wrong—they are, however, not of the same meaning. Good and bad refer to the quality and outcome of an act; right and wrong refer to the means of implementing the good and bad. The close relationship of the two pairs of terms reflects the unitary nature of our conduct where a voluntary act is executed upon deliberation, foresight, choice, and will-effort. Our deliberation and choice may be right or wrong, but the act itself and its consequences are good or bad.

In order to appraise an act morally we must know more than its consequences. We must know its antecedent steps, the physiopsychological make-up of the doer, and the external circumstances which determine it. The choice and the act, the deliberation and execution, the inner states of mind and the outer reality are of equal importance. To judge the outcome alone is to disregard its accidental features which are not of our making; to place the major emphasis on motives, intentions, and foresight is to forget the basic truth that only in acting can we manifest our moral or immoral character.

Good and bad, right and wrong, are contrary terms of moral appraisal with many gradations between them. Neither term is a mere deprivation. The bad is not a negation of the good, nor the good a mere negation of the bad; neither is right the absence of wrong, nor wrong an absence of the right. They symbolize their referents independently of each other, and epitomize realities of a different causative and qualitative nature.

Genetically, good and bad are prior to right and wrong. Because some experiences are satisfying or frustrating, joyful or painful, our reflections center on their generating conditions. The gratifying and frustrating ends call for a scrutiny of their implementing means. Moral ends and moral means are reciprocal, interdependent and interacting elements of our moral consciousness and conscience.

We attribute ethical qualities to our character, not in the sense of a static psychic entity, but rather to traits discernible in action. Honesty, consideration, responsibility, benevolence, and kindness are functional properties. Only in our actual relating of ourselves to our fellow men do we reveal our character. Moral ideas and ideals contemplated in solitude are an asset of the moral life, but, in the final analysis, it is the acting out of them which constitutes the good life.

There is little, if any, disagreement as to the basic or intrinsic ends of man's behavior. Preservation of life, health, security, social participation, opportunities for work and leisure, affection, freedom in all spheres of activity—these are the things men value most. Intrinsic ends reflect our sentient and conative nature. To make them a subject of a rational justification is to misjudge reason in conduct. Man aims at preservation of life. He does not question the value of life as such. This is his biological preference. He questions the different forms of life, the better and worse. He aims at satisfaction of his needs. This satisfaction is not debatable. What is debatable are the various kinds of satisfaction, and the various means he chooses. Needs are beyond justification. We cannot help pursuing them, provided we are physically and mentally healthy. The real ethical problem is to search for a moral order which could do away with tribalistic outlooks, based on the nonrational belief that a single group or nation is better, and hence entitled to an exclusive enjoyment of the good things in life.

Attempts to explain moral right and wrong apart from the basic ends which comprise the good life have led to fruitless discussions. We cannot debate what is right or wrong unless we agree on the good and evil things. The latter are primordial data in ethics. They are indefinable if we look for more familiar terms into which they could be translated. They are definable in a denotative sense by pointing out the instances of gratification and frustration, and genetically by describing their antecedent conditions.

The moral good and bad are satisfactions or frustrations men cause to other men. The right is the fitted for a moral good, the wrong is the unfitted for a moral good or fitted for a moral bad. No action is objectively morally right if its results are detrimental to the well-being of man, although we may exonerate a wrong action for reasons of ignorance, limited foresight, or uncontrollable external circumstances. The ever-changing conditions of social life call for a continuous modification of our notions of right and wrong, a modification contingent on our expanding knowledge, and better control of nature. The combatting of a disease through ritualistic ceremonies was right at a time of magical addictions of men. It is a discernible evil at a time of available knowledge of controlling it. To cite more instances would be to labor the obvious.

A universal moral order would be a mere artifact, a sum total of injunctions superimposed on a nonmoral human nature if it were true that every man seeks only his own satisfaction. The truth is that our own gratifications very often include the satisfactions of other people, that our own personal good is fused with the general good of our fellow men. The preservation and augmenting of our intrinsic values call for preservation and augmenting of intrinsic values of other people. To make man's intrinsic values more sharable than they are is a vital necessity. The failure of given moralities in fulfilling this task stems from many factors. Among them the most damaging is the forsaking of scientific procedures in matters of right and wrong, the fear of tackling controversial issues, and the infantile craving for ultimate solutions in the form of a perennial best. The best is an empty, inarticulate ideal. Only the better has substance in social actualities.[4] There is no ultimacy in the life of truth, but a rewarding adventure in solving given perplexities. The same holds true of the moral right.

CHAPTER IX

ETHICAL RELATIVISM AND OBJECTIVE ETHICS

A critical ethical inquiry begins with given moral beliefs and practices. In no human society, even the most primitive one, do we find unregulated conduct. Certain acts and character traits are praised or condemned. A violation of the given customs and mores is frowned upon everywhere. No man can completely discard customary morals which guarantee a minimum of social cohesion.

To accept customary moral standards as final is to forsake ethical reflection. The most dogmatic supporter of customary morality must admit that customs and mores may become obsolete. A way of doing things may have an accidental success, and may eventuate in a stereotyped response which obstructs an understanding of, and reaction to, a unique, novel situation. In addition, many customs originate "in the edicts of persons in authority"[1] who make their own idiosyncrasies into the law of the land, or defend their own social status behind a sacrosanct custom.

The diversity of moral practices and beliefs is a fact no ethicist can deny. We learn that almost all kinds of conduct have been approved or disapproved. To infer from this variety of morals that there is no standard to adjudicate them in terms of better or worse, right and wrong, is to use the term morality in a vacuous sense. Morality, properly speaking, aims at harmony of individual interests, at mitigating conflicts which stem from man's two-fold nature—his incomplete gregariousness and solitary needs.² An objective ethics asks what given moralities do to sustain and enhance man's quest for a happy, satisfactory life in his social setting.

Morals aim at a socialization and humanization of man. Their success or failure depends on whether or not they take cognizance of the fact that human nature is not a clay to be molded into all possible patterns. There are limitations to enculturation and social conventions. Man's basic needs must be fulfilled if we want to mitigate conflict and curb aggressiveness. Repressed needs make for a very spurious moral order. The essentials of the social life cannot fundamentally differ from the essentials of the good life—a life of growth and fulfillment, materially and spiritually. The regard for others comes from a healthy self-regard which in turn is the function of social acceptance, belonging, and affection. We are bound to quibble about an absolute right or wrong if we neglect the real issue—how to make the essentials of the good life such as economic abundance, artistic and intellectual pursuit, social inclusive relatedness, freedom of thought and speech, more pervasive than they are today, more sharable and more secure.

A satisfactory ethics of human relations which could commend itself to reason and experience must be on constant guard against the human proneness to project particular, socially and culturally conditioned valuations and values as binding upon all men. This justified fear of ethnocentrism is the major factor behind the current vogue of moral relativism. Cognizant of the intolerance and harm caused by ethnocentric, absolute moralities, ethical relativists fall in with the false belief that social relations on a national and international level can be improved by discounting any objective moral standard. But the doctrine of ethical equality of the various moralities does not make for greater social harmony. Our moral ideas and attitudes do not become more rational or human by cultivating a tolerance for moral beliefs and practices which rationalize the existing social evils in their brute and subtle forms. They become more civilized by recognizing these evils as such. An obliteration of good and evil will never do it. The social origin of values does not entail a social validation of values. What validates them are the satisfactions which they epitomize. Social determinants may further or cripple them, but they never constitute them. There are trans-social values which men everywhere cherish.

"The fundamental material needs of human beings are universal, or nearly so. If there is anyone so odd that he prefers to starve when he might have a full stomach, to shiver in the cold when he might be sheltered, to be ravaged with disease when he might be healthy, to be overworked and insecure when he might have work that is neither overanxious nor overwearisome, he is at least so rare a "bird" that he can be left out of account in the building of a world order." [3] Not only physiological needs and their satisfactions, but also psychological and social needs and their gratifications show a great similarity. Affection, companionship, social acceptance and recognition, intellectual and artistic activities are universally cherished values. Ethicists who are not prone to speculations about good and evil, right and wrong, find themselves in the predicament of looking for empirical evidence for a moral order in the same studies of human nature which eschew valuations and values. Cognizant that moral conflicts and perplexities stem from actual situations, the ethicist must avail himself of empirical findings which alone can suggest a moral order whose normative standards will be self-certifying. Standards are not self-certifying because of their logical validity and clarity of language. What justifies them as heuristic, guiding principles is their pragmatic role in mitigating the actual conflicts of human desires, goals, and interests. The various empirical studies of man, although pretending to be value-neutral, supply us with normative notions.⁴ It is modern psychology which furnishes us with the evidence of the high value of a social relation based on love and goodness.⁵ It reveals that most forms of aggression are results of excessive repressions, inhibitions and frustrations. It is modern sociology which gives us valuable insights into the cohesive and destructive social forces. It is modern ecology which reveals mutualism as "the key to higher levels of adaptation and fuller exploitation of the limited sources of the environment by different interlocked parts of the living world." ⁶ Modern psychiatry challenges the view that mental health is a form of social adaptation and adjustment. It puts great emphasis on the inner integration of the individual, on his good sense of reality and values. By dwelling upon the constitutional and developmental make-up of the individual, on his happiness and misery, psychiatry disproves the equation of the good life with the socially approved life. Behind the socially approved institution of prostitution there is a host of unbalanced, unhappy individuals whose self-image is that of a frustrated person; behind the socially approved doctrine of the superiority of a group, nation, or race there lurks a host of mentally disturbed individuals indulging in all kinds of delusions of grandeur.

What calls ethics into being are the clearly discernible evils, the tensions and discords which prevail. Genuine ethical reflections focus on very practical problems of alleviating man's misery and promoting his happiness. Their scientific character depends on how much factual evidence is there to support them. Whether life itself is a worthy good is a question too pretentious for ethics to answer. Man's nature is such that life appears a genuine good, and ethics which aspires to be more than a mere academic subject searches for conditions which enhance life; man is a eudaemonistic creature aiming at an enduring well-being or happiness, and no serious ethics will try to disparage this intrinsic end, but rather will center on the conditions of genuine satisfactions. Man is a freedom loving being, he cherishes the real instances of freedom, freedom from obstacles and freedom of growth, and ethics will dwell upon freedom-generating conditions. The discovery of common values whose implementation men everywhere seek is only the starting point of ethical reflections. The real problem for ethics is to find means and ways of making the good life into a morally good life, that is, into a shareable experience. Two fictitious conditions would make ethics impossible or superfluous: a world replete with values, out there in the world waiting for our grasp, and a world full of deprivations, utterly incongruent with our persisting desires and interests. The struggle for the good things in life disproves the first assumption. Conflict of desires and interests is a concomitant of living. The real and possible social accord disproves the second assumption. A certain amount of harmony of desires and interests is also a concomitant of living. Man's moral actions are directed toward mitigating conflict and promoting accord. Their eminently ethical qualities are neither objectified feelings nor mere individual or social idiosyncrasies which transform facts into values. They are consequences brought about by our own doing. They are facts gaining significance in the context of human interests and goals as efficacies for human satisfaction.

The essence of the good life is an enduring gratification. The essence of the morally good life is a satisfaction which makes for satisfaction of other people. To be inconsiderate, to strive for gratifications of needs at the expense of other people's desires, to make one's joy the suffering of another, to claim privileges for oneself which become burdens of our fellow men—these are the clearly discernible immoral doings. Just as the amoral good is an achievement, so, too, the good moral life is an accomplishment, the result of a struggle against the many immoral promptings to which no man is immune.

"Nature and grace, worth and crude being, mutilate each other at every junction of experience; and the fact that action never more than partially equates the idea of purposes with the coarse realities of nature and life is the reason that action is always and continuously necessary."[7] The ethical order where peace, security, freedom from want and fear become universal, sharable goods is a rational ideal whose implementation is a task contingent upon the growing knowledge of nature and man, and our willingness to apply it. Satisfaction of basic needs is essential for an enduring moral order but not sufficient. Exigencies of living together call for principles of conduct which aim at harmonizing conflicting desires and interests. Such norms of behavior in the form of the moral oughtness are not measured by their soundness in logic, but rather by their pragmatic role in mitigating social conflicts. Their imperative character turns into a self-commending asset if and when they take cognizance of man's quest for a happy life.

The oughtness of the moral right is not less explicable than any non-moral oughtness. All forms of oughtness are predicated on man as a goal seeking being. The ought mediates between our incipient and our overt, executed act. To ask for a self-certified moral ought independent of our total context of desires, emotions and aims is as senseless as to ask for a self-certified nonmoral ought independent of what we are aiming at. We do not approach a perplexing situation which requires actions, a choice of alternative courses, in a cognitive pristine way. There is always behind our response some intellectually cumulative experience, our own and that of other people. The oughtness reflects our learning ability. A successfully tested experience turns into an immediately felt requiredness in executing a new act. A successfully applied method of resolving perplexities becomes a directive ought. The skillful mechanic, the rigorous logician, the expert physician—they all draw from the invaluable repository of oughts and ought-nots. A way of acting which turns into a failure becomes an ought-not. There is nothing mysterious about the innumerable oughts and ought-nots which mediate between our drives, interests, goals, and our responses. They are essential parts of the total structure of purposive acts. They figure as right and wrong standards in the attainment of a purposive goal.[8] Their derivation from the facts of social behavior is beyond question. We cannot help going after pleasant experiences and avoiding unpleasant ones. The rationality or irrationality of the moral oughts rests with their fulfilling or frustrating functions. The derivation of an ought-requiredness is not a logical inference which requires an ought premise to justify an ought conclusion. The derivation of an ought has its roots in our physiological and psychological make-up. No logical inference is possible and necessary in convincing us that we ought not drink a poisonous liquid. From the fact that it is poisonous does not follow that we ought not drink it. The ought rests with our conative nature, with our will to live. If the moral ought is not based on or suggested by the facts of social accord and discord, it remains a thin, lifeless entity. Experimenting in living together leads to a selection of ways of acting. Those which make for greater social cohesion and harmony become obligatory, insistent elements of our moral experience. This is one part of the moral ought. Its second part, the aspirational or ideal ought rests with man's ability to gain from each fact a new, possible fact. Every given attainment suggests a new, a better, a more efficient one. Where elementary moral oughts are lacking, the higher moral oughts have no chance of becoming a salient feature of our moral conscience or consciousness.

The higher forms of goodness are predicated on impulses and interests which are free from the tension of unfulfilled physiological needs. Our urge to relate ourselves to our fellow men in the most inclusive way, our need for giving and receiving affection, our creative constructive faculties remain dormant or crippled when our basic desires are frustrated.

There is little disagreement as to the high and low, better or worse of the technological aspect of culture. Here the standard is the conquest and control of natural forces for the benefit of human needs. We do judge a given culture higher which reduces the struggle for the necessities of existence and makes for a life of enhancement instead of a mere subsistence. But when it comes to questions of the moral right and wrong we embrace a relativistic point of view which equates the moral right and wrong with what a given society or culture approves or disapproves. Ethical relativism is presented to us as a scientific theory based on anthropological studies of various societies and cultures. These, we learn, approve and disapprove most antithetical conducts. Historical evidence for a gamut of different contradictory morals is given. So, too, a historical evidence for a vast medley of various, contradictory outlooks on nature. And yet no physicist will use this evidence for a scientific relativism which would equate truth and falsehood with what a given society approves or disapproves. Its ascertained truth and workability are the decisive criteria, and not social validation. An irrational, magical outlook on nature is inferior to an outlook based on experience and reason irrespective of societal forces, because the latter helps us to implement our basic aims—reduction of fear of the unknown and harnessing natural energies for human needs. Just as the physical outlook of primitive man is ineffective because of its underlying superstitions, so, too, his moral outlook is ineffective because of the irrational beliefs related to means and ways of implementing the good life.

"Most of the disagreements that occur in practice are, not as to what things have intrinsic value, but as to who shall enjoy them. The holders of power naturally demand for themselves the lion's share. Disagreements of this sort tend to become mere contests for power. In theory, this sort of question can be decided by our general criterion: that system is best which produces a maximum of intrinsic value. Disputes may remain when both sides accept this criterion, but they then have become disputes as to fact and will be, at least in theory, amenable to scientific treatment." [9]

The political and social turmoil of our age makes us despair of a common humanity. But a critical appraisal of these turmoils reveals a very encouraging truth that the major cause of the recurrent conflicts is not the absence of common values, but rather a biased application of these values. People everywhere crave for the same goods but in their tribalistic outlook do not consider everyone entitled to the same goods. Current ideologies rationalize the biased application of values as a diversity of incompatible values. They either project the moral tribalism as an unalterable fact or pit one parochial ideology against another one.

Ideological disputes are opaque to reason. They have their roots in sentiments, fixated illusions, power interests, and social pressures. Not so theories. By appealing to reason and experience, the only genuine sources of knowledge, to public methods of observation, verification, and critical requirements of sound thinking they can be checked and rechecked as to their truth. While theories enrich our knowledge, ideologies do not. They do not solve perplexing problems, but sidetrack them. Like myths they are projections of passions and illusions, nourished by a spurious sense of certainty and finality. What makes them more damaging than a myth is their pseudoscientific character. A genuine myth is a poetic attempt to reduce the tensions the unknown engenders. Ideologies misconstrue the known and knowable. They amass facts which fit into their preconceived framework and omit facts which belie their main assumptions. They appeal to passions prone to irrational panaceas, and blind us to the vital distinction between wishes and workable ideals. Wishes thrive on fancy, ideals on a good sense of reality. Wishes make our imagination and intellect subservient to emotions and passions, ideals check the latter as to their rationality. They call for constructive efforts of will and intelligence in the arduous process of implementing desirable goals suggested by concrete, scrutinized actualities and conditions of social living.

As in the past, so too in the present, ideologies get hold of men because of their strange mixture of facts and fancy, valid reasoning and glaring inconsistencies. Plato is a case in point. Reading his Republic we are moved by the logic of discourse, by the quest for justice which differentiates between might and right. But behind the beauty and structure of his ideas there is the ugly myth of immutable, rigid classes. Man, Plato tells us, is born either a ruler, a guardian, or worker. The divine being ordained this inequality by creating some people of gold, some of silver, and some of brass. Plato himself is aware of the mythological, noble lie. He argues that man can be easily inculcated with this myth in no more than two generations. In the course of years the myth turns into a free acceptance, an internalized social custom. Plato is right in what he has to say about enculturation. The bloody human record attests the power of ideological creeds which could never reach such dimensions of cruelty and callousness if not for their encultured hold of man's mind and emotions. But Plato is wrong in fancying a real social eudaemonia based on an arbitrary distortion of man's genuine values centering on his emotional and intellectual growth or self-realization. Justice in the sense of an harmonious individual and social integration, of a moral order of pervasive human happiness cannot be decreed or stipulated. It must be discovered in the actualities of social living in the same manner as laws of nature are discovered by patient observations of facts and bold hypothetical projections suggested by an unbiased study of facts. Such a moral order will belie the ethnocentrism of the various ideologies. With the replacement of the latter by warranted knowledge "humanity may discover for itself a common language and common values. When ideologies recede, it will be the ebbtide of human hatreds, and the energies of men, disenthralled from conflict and suppression, will know new horizons of happiness and achievement." [10]

An objective ethics is predicated on common values which may take different forms in the life of a single individual or group. Universality of values does not entail a uniformity of values. Life would be a very dull affair if everyone craved for or aspired to identical values. Universal, common values allow for endless designs whose essential properties will be the same. No matter on what intrinsic ends we reflect —health, affection, beauty, intelligence, satisfying work, loyalty,—as consummatory values they differ from individual to individual, from one group to another. They differ in degree, not in kind. Universality of values and diversity of cultures are complementary. The greatest cultural diversity is to be found among nations which allow for a fulfillment of basic values. Where the latter are crippled, a cultural stagnation is the result.

Objectivity of values should not be confused with a value absolutism. Just as an absolute truth, an eternal entity independent of man is beyond articulation and comprehension, so, too, an absolute value is inconceivable. No matter in which field, the process of knowing and appreciating is not a passive mirroring of things and events, but rather an interaction of a perceiving and thinking subject and a perceived, known object. Knowledge is related to man, to his ways of perceiving, feeling and understanding. Given beings of a different sensuality and reason, reality is bound to be different. Known and appreciated phenomena are relational phenomena. Being relational phenomena truth and values are subject to change. This change may be of two kinds; a truth turned into falsehood, or a truth becoming larger, more inclusive; a value turned into a disvalue, or a value becoming more inclusive. This historical relativism of truth and value does not preclude objectivity in the sense of intersubjective, impersonal, intersocial and intercultural truth and value. There is one physics, one biology, and one chemistry. Here the impersonal truth is based on ascertained facts and methods of verification. When it comes to values, especially moral values, the good and evil, right and wrong, disagreements are frequent, not so much for the difficulty of the issues, but rather for artificial barriers. One of these is our urge for certainty and finality in matters of morality. Out of this urge speculations about absolute values and a denial of the cognitive status of values come into being. The fact that truth changes is not taken as a case for its relativism. The fact that our values change is taken as a case for value subjectivism or social relativism. Man as a perceiving being supplies the data for an abstract conceptual framework called physics; man as a sentient being supplies the data for an abstract conceptual framework called ethics. Drop perceptions and the distinction between truth and falsehood disappears. Drop the sentient being and the distinction between good and evil loses its meaning.

We could probably advance more rapidly toward a satisfactory ethics of human relations if we desist from looking for norms of conduct binding upon all men, the normal and abnormal, the moral and immoral, the social and criminal alike. The norm which enjoins us to treat every human being as an equal, subject to the same fulfillments and frustrations, to the same vicissitudes of the precarious human existence, to weigh the weal and woe of others with whom we interact, can never be binding upon socially and mentally deranged people. These are proper subjects of psychological and medical studies. In our moral discourses we too often neglect the specific requirements of any sensible discourse and engage in discussion with people who are in dire need of moral training in the essentials of living together.

CHAPTER X

SCIENCE AND ETHICS

The invention and spread of nuclear weapons threatening to destroy mankind makes us aware of the vital issue: the impact of science on values. In the absence of a critical, dispassionate elucidation of this urgent problem, people move from one extreme to another—from a vehement accusation of science and what it stands for, to its uncritical acceptance; from skepticism as to the authority of science in the realm of values, to dogmaticism as to its role in verification and validation of man's genuine ends. Those who attack science are in a majority. The attacks are not confined to natural sciences. More and more people voice their discontent with contemporary studies of man—psychology, sociology, and psychiatry—which try to unravel the overt and hidden dynamics of social living.

Most scientists respond to these attacks with unconcern or with the comforting answer that science is supreme in the field of instrumental values, but incompetent in the realm of intrinsic ends and goals men choose to implement. Science, so runs the argument, can make a desert bloom or turn a cultivated garden into a desert; it can employ nuclear energies for constructive or destructive purposes; it can cure a disease or spread it. This dichotomy of means and ends, instrumental and intrinsic values, so plausible on the surface, disregards the continuum of means and ends in human conduct. Here ends may become means, and means may become ends.[1] A critical appraisal of means may make the end more or less desirable, and the desirability of an end may bring forth greater efforts in procuring proper means.

We like to attribute any step forward in the process of humanizing social relations to a few moral pioneers whose sensitivity to man's misery and suffering has inspired their vision of a better, more dignified life. But notwithstanding the efforts of these valiant men, it has been science which has accelerated the humanizing process by narrowing the gap between brute facts and ideals, between a life of mere subsistence and an enhanced life. Moral resentment and indignation are effective forces behind any step forward. Science nurtures these forces by giving them efficacies. Scientific discoveries which have taught us to cultivate the soil, to control the physical environment, to combat disease, to substitute machines for hard manual work, have been mitigating the struggle for existence, and have thus liberated more humane feelings. In the final analysis, it will be science which will make the good things in life more pervasive than they are today. It will be a scientific economy which will hasten the conquest of a parochial, ethnocentric morality by a universal ethos.

The growing global orientation is the moral legacy of contemporary science which brings to a better awareness the oneness of mankind. With the rapid advance of technology, transportation and communication, the affairs of one country become a part of another one. What happens in remote regions enters our consciousness in a very vivid way. No nation can be indifferent to the weal and woe of other nations. Neither can a nation indulge in the most demoralizing myth of racial superiority. The more we learn about cultural achievements of people everywhere, their similar and different ways of life, the less can we afford a tribal attitude of seclusion and isolation. We know that economic prosperity and depression are global phenomena. Even the most prosperous nation is not economically independent. International commerce is a great humanizing factor. It brings people together, and thus eliminates preconceived biases. Scientific advances are of international character. The conquest of diseases, the ever expanding knowledge of the structure of matter and energy are results of constructive efforts of many nations. The same holds true of great literary and artistic works which transcend national, religious, and racial boundaries.

Man's urge to know is intimately bound up with his desire to improve his struggle for survival, and to enhance his life. What keeps our intellectual curiosity alive is the joy of knowing whenever we penetrate into the structure and interconnections of things and events. The known stops being a mere contemplated object. It enters into the context of our impulses, needs, desires, and aspirations. As such it is viewed in terms of its efficacies, actual potential value properties. We do not investigate or care for facts as such, rather we study facts for their valuational implications.

While science is primarily predicated on the urge to know, ethics stems from our desire to avail ourselves of the given knowledge in securing, promoting, and augmenting the objects of gratifications which comprise the good life. Both needs are complementary. The present divorce of science from ethics, factual judgments from value judgments, neglects the unitary nature of man as a knowing and acting individual. Our likes and dislikes are constantly modified by the cognitive grasp of the objects. Contrary to the widespread belief, science did not come of age at a time of a complete discarding of values, but rather at a time of a value reconstruction, of a transition from nonrational, customary moral commitments to a mature, reflective morality which adjudicates man's common aspirations, centering on the good life in the light of their feasibilities.

There are intrinsic moral values without which any genuine science ceases to exist or grow—adherence to truth, to public methods of its verification and norms of validity, to an unobstructed freedom of research, to a militant vigilance against ignorance and superstition, to the value of free communication and dissemination of truth. Where science violates these intrinsic moral values, it becomes subservient to a political ideology with a glaring perversion of truth as an end result. The unfailing search for truth, the live nerve of science is predicated on an ethically oriented society which cherishes freedom of thought, speech, assembly, and is loath to artificial barriers of race, nationality, and creed. Science cannot thrive in the long run in an atmosphere where good and bad, right and wrong are obliterated. Its very existence depends upon valuational decisions in terms of a common, human good and right. Parochialism in morality is detrimental to preservation and augmenting of knowledge of the nature of man and of the world in which he lives.

Science has not been neutral to man's basic values which evolve around preservation and enhancement of life. No matter what scientific field we reflect upon, these values are the driving forces behind any noticeable advance. It is not preservation of sickness, but its eradication which makes for medical advancements; it is not preservation of physical evils such as famine, droughts, and floods, but their conquest, which pushes physical sciences ahead; it is not preservation of social conflicts, but the attempt to mitigate them which accounts for the growing knowledge related to man's mainsprings of action and his social relations. Science cannot be neutral to these basic values which are predicated on the fundamental commitment that the human race is worthy of being preserved and elevated. The continuation of science stands or falls with this commitment.

History of science is a living testimony to the continuity

of knowledge and value. With every gain of knowledge its usage for the benefit of mankind raises a moral problem. Events detrimental to man's quest for happiness are physical phenomena as long as they cannot be controlled or changed. Famine which is beyond our control is not an ethical datum, but a famine which can be checked is. The same holds true of other instances of evil—sickness, premature death, social strifes, wars, etc. To know their causes and remedies and not to change them is a moral transgression. Ethics adds to the scientific purpose to know "the practical motive to control, and it is the latter motive that distinguishes it from sciences and makes it the basis of all the cultural disciplines. Ethics then represents man's efforts to make over the world on a basis of a knowledge of it and in accordance with his wishes and purposes. This motive to reconstruct the world is the ethical motive properly so called, and this ethical motive becomes the central feature in the cultural disciplines of politics, law, religion, and art. It involves thus both the motive to know and the motive to control, and it is not always easy to distinguish the one from the other."[2] A rational ethics which commends itself to reason and experience adjudicates given moralities in terms of the good life they affirm, preserve and augment. It looks upon the instances of the good and evil as real occurrences and not just as conditioned responses to value-free phenomena. They are actualities a given culture may rationalize away, but in the long run they assert and reassert themselves as real events. Just as sociology of knowledge related to nature has been replaced by the sciences of nature which adhere to transocial and transcultural criteria of truth and validity, so, too, the sociology of the good life, underlying the current moral relativism will be superseded by the science of the good life. There was a time, and not a very distant one, when various societies were arbitrators of physical and mental health. Today the number of people who disregard pertinent, objective knowledge related to both is fast declining. They realize that physical and mental health are not mere forms of adjustment that a given society prescribes and sanctions. In reality, they are instances of organic and psychological integration, caused by many factors—disturbance of the biochemical equilibrium, injuries to the organs, and a mode of life out of the context with reality. Men may decree what social accord or discord is (as many utopias of constructive or destructive nature have done), but the real accord and discord will not be arbitrated at will, it will be discovered in the actualities of social living.

An objective ethics stands or falls with the proof or disproof of universal human values. Since ethical relativists and ethical objectivists appeal to the same moral and immoral data, their difference rests on a various interpretation of the implicit and explicit valuations and values underlying social relations. If we identify the moral and immoral with that which a given society approves or disapproves (the essence of ethical relativism) the good and evil, right and wrong become accidental phenomena of a transitory enculturation. There would be no such person as the moral or immoral individual without regard to the society or culture to which he belongs. The cannibal would be moral in a cannibalistic society, immoral in a society which condemns cannibalism; the rapist moral in a community indulging and approving rape, immoral in a group which forbids rape. Parents subjecting their children to violence and most cruel treatment would be moral in a community which accepts and fosters such practices, immoral in a group which frowns upon such behavior as a crime; the rabble rouser who incites masses against other people would be moral if such agitation is sanctioned in the name of the superiority of the white race or class, immoral if the law of the land and the moral code of the people forbid it. This perversion of moral values is presented to us as a result of a scientific approach to morals. In reality, it is the subtlest form of forsaking science and all that it stands for in matters of human relations. It assumes (contrary to facts) that the good and evil can be arbitrated at will without regard for man's bio-chemical, psychological, and social makeup. The latter resists forms of socialization and enculturation which are hostile to it, and belies the naive belief that there is no way of telling which social order gives a satisfactory answer to the problem of human existence.[3]

Human history is not only a bloody record of blind and destructive passions, but also to a large extent a struggle for implementing basic needs in the form of intrinsic, common values; a struggle for survival and enhancement of life, free from fears and hostilities; a strife for freedom, justice and decency for all. Ethical and cultural relativism came into being as a vigorous movement against the prevailing ethical and cultural parochialism which has bred false pride of ethnocentricity, based on the infantile belief that a single group or society is better than any other. This non-rational belief cannot successfully be fought by showing that all moral values are relative, by claiming that we do not have a yardstick to measure an objective right and wrong. Ethical relativism fortifies the same parochialism it intends to eradicate, for it entails an acquiescence in whatever morality prevails in a given society, an attitude of moral indifference to the physical and psychical forms of aggression which are committed under the disguise of socially accepted values, immune to any criticism.

Theoretically we can afford to be skeptics or relativists concerning the real and the valuable or worthy of pursuit. Not so in our daily living which is predicated on certain objective constituents of both. The real differs from the merely imaginary or subjective by having consequences whose neglect may spell the difference between being alive and dead. The genuinely valuable differs from wishful imputed values by having the same feature. Since the dawn of civilization there have been men who did not accept the complacent belief that whatever prevails in a society is good and right. Tyranny, deprivations of body and mind, limitations of growth, social and religious barriers have been for them instances of evil, regardless of the social approval which has sanctioned these evils. The saints of different societies and cultures, the great artists or various milieus, and great scientists all over the world who have fought ignorance and superstition, have bequeathed upon us the vision of a common humanity for which the empirical evidence has been obscured, ignored or misinterpreted. Beneath the moral and cultural differences there is a common bio-social nature of man which can be fulfilled or frustrated. The better or worse, the right and wrong measure the degrees of fulfillment or frustration. Empirical studies disclose common human needs and aspiration. Science helps us to detect the concrete goods and evils, and supplies us with means of implementing the first and remedying the second. It does not prove the moral oughtness, the binding recognition of the rightness of man's needs and aspirations. The fact that men everywhere crave for the good things in life does not entail the moral ought which admonishes us to recognize and respect man's rights to them. The moral ought is our moral commitment. It reflects the kind of personality we are, and the kind of society we belong to. Our moral commitments are neither true nor false. They are rational or non-rational, useful or useless. They are indicators of our reasonableness and our willingness to learn from experience. Experiments in living together teach us that our own values are preserved and augmented in a social setting where the values of other people are preserved and augmented; that the satisfying life (materially and spiritually) of one group is bound up with another group, that freedom of one man entails the freedom of all, that a parochial justice is a misnomer. Continual strifes of civil and international nature feed on man's parochial moral outlook that one individual or group is better than any other one. This infantile belief is fortified with all kinds of rationalizations that there are superior races or nations, that the natural inequality of man entails an inequality of rights, that might can make anything into right, and that man is the arbitrator or measure of good and evil. Matters of fact, it is true, do not prove the moral ought which guides our conduct. But they can tell us a great deal about the rationality or irrationality of our moral commitments. If we commit ourselves to the freedom of a few, history teaches us that such a freedom is very precarious; if we restrict civil rights to a small group, the arbitrariness in excluding other people penalizes us for we are in danger of becoming victims of inequal rights and partisan justice. Where partiality colors our moral commitments and judgments, the two sets of values, one for ourselves and one for others, the inconsistent and contradictory standards are behind our poor self-integration and social adjustment. A double standard of values for the nearest and the remote, the in-group and the out-group, makes not only one and the same situation ambivalent, but what counts more, it does not allow our constructive feelings and interests to expand fully. It makes for love with hatred, admiration with contempt. It feeds conflicts which use up energies which could be put to better purposes. Very little productive energy is left in persons who are perturbed by antagonistic feelings, conceit, fear, or guilt reactions.

The quest for a universal morality has perplexed many ethicists since Socrates refused to accept the sweeping generalities advanced by the Sophists that might makes anything into right, might as the prerogative of the stronger individual or as sheer power of the masses. Although Socrates himself, and Plato and Aristotle have bestowed upon us a rich legacy of moral wisdom, their ethical framework is vulnerable to many salient objections. Most of all, they made excessive claims for reason as a guide to action. Their appraisal of impulses and passions shows an intellectualistic bias. Instead of realizing the balancing nature of our sensuous, conative, and cognitive faculties, they wrongly separated the cognitive ability, and made it supreme. Apart from the moral intellectualism, the Greek philosophers neglected entirely the historical approach to morals which would have shown to them a development of moral ideas in concatenation with the general growth of ideas. Their notion of an unchangeable summum bonum is the result of the lacking genetic approach. In no field of human inquiry is there any ultimacy. Knowledge is steadily evolving. With good and evil it is not different from the knowledge of reality. Both have a history conditioned by many factors—refinements of the methods of observation and experimentation; the replacement of derivative sources of knowledge by reason and experience; the change of the social climate which may be conducive or detrimental to an unbiased research. An objective ethics has nothing to fear from a genetic, empirical study of morals in their total configuration. Such an approach does not prove that man's notions of right and wrong are solely determined by societal forces which may enforce a certain behavior as right. Even the most dogmatic advocate of the social approbative theory[4] cannot avoid using a standard which contradicts his main assertion that customs are always right, for he cannot help adjudicating customs in terms of social expedience, and by doing it, must realize that customs and mores may have a nonrational origin. Furthermore, the social approbative theory of morals disregards the blatant fact that each civil community comprises various groups which may have different standards from those of the majority. Any dissenter from the powerful majority group would become immoral. "The issue comes to a head in determining the proper ethical evaluation of a social reformer. Many of the great heroes of political history are the successful social reformers—Pericles, Marc Anthony, Cromwell, Washington—or the martyrs to causes which come to be approved—Buddha, Socrates, Jesus, Thomas More. These men were nonconformists, and by the theory of the cultural relativist were all bad men." [5]

Morals, no doubt, are social. Man in isolation is not moral or immoral. Moral practices and beliefs develop in a social medium, just as science, art, and religion do. What gives rise to morality are the innumerable exigencies of living together, similar situations, common frustrations and fulfillments. But the social origin of morals should not be confused with a social validation of morals. The good and evil we cherish and abhor are real events. The test of a value or disvalue is not different from the test of any material entity—its ascertained function, its regularity in occurrence, and predictive consequences. The objective right and wrong stand for satisfactory or unsatisfactory solutions to man's existence. Since the desirable forms of the good life undergo a steady modification as we advance in our knowledge of nature and man, a continual criticism of moral principles, embedded in tradition and customs, is a vital necessity. Such a criticism cannot go beyond good and evil. As a social being, living in a community, man has no choice of accepting or rejecting the moral life, for without certain basic agreements and norms of conduct communal life will cease. Our choice is between morals which minister to our needs and goals in a rational, efficient way, and morals which have lost their usefulness. Moral habits and customs are a great asset against individual arbitrariness in judging something as good and bad, right and wrong. But they must be modified in the light of new findings related to man's happiness and misery. Life itself places the highest premium on principles of conduct which take proper care of the actual forces of social accord and discord.

A contemporary ethicist finds himself in a peculiar position. If he makes statements describing the intricacies of human motivation, he is regarded as a psychologist; if he dwells upon the causes of social accord and discord, he is classified as a sociologist; if he analyzes the moral language, he is a semanticist or logician; if he appraises given moral beliefs and practices in terms of an objective standard or tries to distinguish between true and spurious values centering on the notion of the good life, he is accused of being a metaphysician who deals with meaningless, pseudo-concepts.[6] This not flattering characterization comes from positivistic and analytic schools of thought which accept Hume's distinction between matters of fact and relations of ideas as a final one. Matters of fact refer to synthetical a posteriori propositions which comprise all empirical sciences. Relations of ideas refer to analytical a priori propositions of mathematics and logic. Synthetical propositions are contingent upon experience. Their truth or falsity is based on facts. Analytical propositions have no empirical content. They elucidate the meanings of words and their relations. Since our value judgments do not fit into any of these categories, they are dismissed as meaningless, or sentences containing emotive words, devoid of any cognitive meaning.

Hume's dichotomy between matters of fact and relations of ideas has turned many ethicists into skeptics who deny the possibility of an objective ethics; into analysts who confine ethics to a study of the moral language or meta-ethical excursions; into naturalists who obliterate the distinction between matters of fact and value judgments; and ethical intuitionists who claim a unique, cognitive status for value judgments.

Value judgments are descriptive and prescriptive at the same time, predicated on facts and appraising facts. This two-fold role is a unique feature of value judgments, which usually are instances of mixed functions of language—expressive, evocative, and informative. The nature of value judgments is certainly a difficult and perplexing issue, but by no means an unsolvable problem if we realize the main purposes of value assertions: how well an object, event or behavior answers to our needs, purposes and expectations. They are bound up with descriptive factual statements but not identical with them. To call a deed good or evaluate man's character as good means much more than enumerating a few facts. It means at the same time to appraise these facts in the light of a moral standard. The latter is our moral commitment which can be rational or irrational, feasible or unfeasible, useful or useless. Once we agree on the moral end or standard, scientific findings, related to our knowledge of nature and man, gain moral significance. Placed in the context of human desires and aspirations, they help us to implement our moral commitments and change them in the light of their ascertained feasibility.

Choosing an end is a moral commitment, deliberation upon alternative ends is an ethical reflection. Both, if rational, are predicated on scientific knowledge. Thus ethics is contingent upon science. That science in turn is contingent upon ethics is not less true, although not widely recognized today. If the ends for which science supplies the necessary means are chosen by people who lack moral wisdom and are callous to man's quest for a happy life, science which claims to be neutral as to the ultimate human values, may crowd itself out of existence. Science cannot and should not be neutral to the most basic end that human life is worth being preserved. It is the same intrinsic end which gave rise to science, and the same end will be decisive for its continual growth.

CHAPTER XI

ETHICS AND RELIGION

The origin, history, and ubiquity of religion give a vivid testimony to man's genuine need for a synoptic view of nature, and man's place in it. Such a view is never content with given scientific achievements, no matter how far back they may push the realm of the unknown. Questions such as the purpose and meaning of life, human destiny, the riddles of being in general, and the mystery of human existence in particular, surpass the domain of science. They are essential religious issues whose solutions require some leap into the unknown. To ask whether religion is necessary for an ethics which could commend itself to reason and experience, and command a universal appeal, is as senseless as asking whether art is vital to it. Man cannot help pursuing artistic and religious activities. They are salient features of his very existence in its real and ideal dimensions. No matter how much knowledge we may gain about the structure and interconnections of events, there will always be some inexplainable, perplexing problem which calls for a nonempirical belief or faith which transcends the known and knowable. To a certain extent science itself is predicated on faith. Its major axiomatic assumptions go beyond empirical evidence. Our true and valid generalizations are contingent upon a uniform and orderly nature. The belief that this order will prevail is only partially justified empirically. By making inferences from the regularities of the past to the regularities of the future we believe that the universe will remain an orderly process, a uniform nexus of causes and effects. Such a belief has elements of a religious faith. The latter lives in our hopes and expectations that the unknown phenomenon of today will be the known of tomorrow, that our efforts to eradicate sickness, poverty, and ignorance will not be in vain. Our hopes are predicated on the explicit or implicit belief that the universe in which we live is not opaque or hostile to our aspirations.

Contrary to popular opinions, true science does not discard faith, but gives it a better foundation. "The more we know, the deeper reasons we find for feeling our insignificance and littleness in the vast universe. The geocentric world outlook was awe-inspiring. Still more the discovery that our earth is only a tiny body among millions of others. Our sense of humility and dependence was not weakened, rather strengthened by the revelation of the immense energies of nature."[1]

Religious values grow with other values. A coalescence of values, and not a substitution of values makes for an enhanced, gratifying life. Material values without spiritual values, or spiritual values without material values are not conducive to a social cohesion of a full self-realization, and effective cooperation. Genuine religious values play an important role in the cultivation of social feelings such as pity, sympathy, understanding of our fellow men as equals in the brief and precarious sojourn our life means. Most of all, a true religion will never fail to remind us how frail we are in our solitary, amoral, and immoral existence. Faith in one form or another, faith in a transcending and transcendent God, or perpetuating human spirit in its cultural continuity, faith in dignity of man, faith in ideals which add zest for living, is essential to procure and augment the good life of growth. "Not out of hybris, contentment, did science grow, but out of felt and apprehended shortcomings, insufficiencies;

and religious values point to these with the same vigor as other values do. Not the sodden and bloated impostors, wicked tyrants who thought of themselves as omnipotent masters, liberated man from darkness, but the creative, modest geniuses who suffered with the human lot and saw behind man's omnipotence a misguided impotence. Humility before God should not be confused with humility before man. Piety, reverence, worship attached to frail and abject ends become irreligious expressions. It is the nature of the objective which renders our emotions religious or irreligious." [2]

Socio-cultural conditions determine the kind of religion we cherish but not the fact that we have religion. The latter is nurtured by certain emotive, conative, and cognitive elements which transcend given social, economic, and political determinants. It is not a single impulse or feeling which goes into the making of religion, but a cluster of impulses and feelings: wonder, awe, reverence, gratitude, fear of the unknown, the consciousness of our finitude, the transient and enduring anxieties of our existence, the need for security and dependence in a world full of precariousness and contingencies.

The historical development of religion reveals an intimate relationship of emotive and cognitive factors. Religious feelings, like moral feelings, change with the growth of cognitive ideas. Knowledge has an impact on them. Social pressures and institutional forces may slight this impact, but in the long run no living religion can remain aloof from, or immune to, any scientific advance. At a time when our knowledge of nature was in its infancy, a frightening, unknown universe engendered the belief in a diffuse power operating in all events concerning man: health, sickness, crops, birth, drought, growth, and decay. From worshipping of this mysterious power man has moved to animism and spiritism. The prevailing patterns of worshipping on these stages are magical or ritual incantations designed to propitiate the various deities. Polytheistic religions have been superseded by monotheistic beliefs, centering on the notion of a sublime, divine power, either in the form of a spiritual person or an indefinite, spiritual, all-pervasive entity. Whereas primitive stages of religious development reflect man's preoccupation with fertility cults related to the physical necessities of living, religion in its advanced stages has as its dominant theme the betterment of social relations.[3]

Like science and art, religion epitomizes values which transcend boundaries of race and nationality. The images and symbols it employs express common strivings, anxieties, and exaltations.[4] The fatherhood of God, the essential tenet of all major living religions, articulates the unity of mankind, in its hereditary constitution and salient features of existence. The socio-cultural differences fade into insignficance as compared to man's basic needs and aspirations. It is not so much the conflict of the latter which divides man, as the biased value orientation, the false pride that one is better than the other, and thus entitled to a better life. The fatherhood of God is a forceful reminder of the still untapped pool of spiritual resources of various nations and races whose cooperative sharing could successfully counteract the divisive forces of political ideologies. What stands in the way of a better humanity is not the irrational destructive human nature, but the corrosive effects of ideologies which deceive man as to his place in nature, as to his basic life-sustaining values.

Religious and moral transgressions go hand in hand. A self-centered life, bent on exploitation and humiliation of others, follows from morbid illusions and delusions that an individual can find integration apart from other people and apart from the world. The root of obligation or duty, so central to communal life, is the sound awareness of how much we owe to others in our continuous struggle for survival. Genuine religion fosters this essential feeling by reminding us that we ought not to take the good things in life for granted. Science can teach us the conditions of the good life, but we need faith that these conditions are within our reach and that they will continue to be in our control.

CHAPTER XII

ON MORAL PROGRESS
TOWARD A UNIVERSAL ETHOS

Prior to the Age of Reason or Enlightenment, the idea of progress was unknown. The prevalent outlook on nature in general, and man's place in it, was a static and fatalistic one. Truth, no matter in which field, was thought of as an immutable, absolute entity, out there in the world, to be grasped by reason or intuition. It was predicated on a universe where all forms of inorganic and organic matter, once brought into being by a divine power or cosmic intelligence, remain the same. Concerning man's destiny, a series of cyclical designs, ordained in advance and beyond man's control, was the prevailing pattern. Men were supposed to move from a golden age of peace, contentment and happiness to less happy stages, the silver and bronze stages. From the latter they could move back to the golden age through divine grace or an inexplicable, ironclad law of nature.

The static view of nature and the cyclical interpretation of human history reflect a deep-seated pessimism which has paralyzed any higher aspiration for a social reconstruction. The latter was rejected as impious and impossible. The best man could do was to accept his fate with fortitude. Small wonder that the ethical reflections of the Greeks and Romans, of the great religious innovators and humanitarians centered more on the inner states of mind than on external conditions.

But by viewing mankind as subject to a universal destiny they encouraged the persisting quest for an ethos which derives its universal code from man's very existence, his common needs and aspirations, fears and anxieties, joys and sorrows.

With the advance of natural sciences the idea of progress gained momentum. The cumulative body of knowledge increased man's power over nature. The confidence in reason working in conjunction with observation was the finest legacy of the Age of Enlightenment. While the Greek philosophers glorified reason as man's greatest asset, their espoused reason was a passive, contemplative organ, revolving about an unchangeable, eternal truth. The reason the Age of Enlightenment glorifies is an active faculty searching for an evolving truth which studies facts in order to make them subservient to our needs and goals. Known and knowable facts are viewed as actual and potential efficacies for a better, enhanced life.

That man's misery rests to a high extent on his ignorance, was the immortal insight of Plato. But he equated ignorance with a preoccupation with the world of phenomena or appearances. According to him, genuine wisdom centers on the realm of ideas as non-spatial and non-temporal essences or entities. Since change is a feature of the realm of phenomena, it was looked upon as an evil. Man's moral progress, if any, was a matter of meditating and contemplating an eternal good the proper thinking of which would automatically bring about a proper acting.

Although there is no unanimity among the thinkers of the Age of Reason concerning the idea of progress, they all share certain convictions: that the cumulative knowledge of nature has feasible implications for a social reconstruction toward a more humane and more dignified political and moral state of affairs; that nature is benign and tractable to man's aspirations; that man's aggressiveness is more a function of environmental conditions than an innate trait; that reason in conjunction with experience is in a position to disclose invariant laws upon which we can build a rational moral order; that dissemination of knowledge has favorable repercussions on fixated and irrational attitudes and beliefs; that man has perfectibility, not in an unlimited sense, but in accordance with his potentialities, which a proper education can channel toward greater sociability and rationality. For the majority of thinkers of the Age of Reason the notion of an inevitable progress is a nonrational one, for social reform and inevitability of progress are contradictory assertions. Inevitable progress is a tenet of historical ideologies set forth by Hegel and Marx who view man as an instrument of impersonal forces which defy genuine creativity. For Hegel these forces are personified as a universal spirit, for Marx they are economic values, the production and distribution of economic goods. Man through his own effort and intelligence may hasten progress but cannot prevent it. The idea of an inevitable progress has revived the old myth of an inevitable cycle of human history, and brought about the new myth of the inevitable decline of human civilization (Spengler). Inevitable progress and inevitable decline are ideological assertions disguised as theories of man. Man's designs of living are to a high degree of his own making. He may use his knowledge and ingenuity for constructive or destructive purposes, for establishing a moral order or chaos, for a life of expanding happiness or increasing misery. That human history repeats itself often is a sad fact. That it must repeat itself is an untenable belief fed on ignorance, stupidity, and callousness.

Man had to go a long way to use the vast repository of trials and errors, successes and failures of the past in arriving at the solid, warranted knowledge of nature. In his political, social, and moral problems he does not use tradition as a storehouse of ideas which fructify new ideas, but rather as a substitute for new thinking and experimenting, as if every new situation and perplexity had some precedent which could be imitated or repeated blindly. Not more rational is the other extreme of the passionate, fanatical reformer who breaks completely with the past. Genuine solutions to vital, perplexing issues, are not random guesses discontinuous with the past. Much of the disillusionment which followed the Age of Reason rests on the exaggerated claims of its zestful reformers who would like to build a future without the follies of the past, and without the wisdom of the past.

We cannot sensibly speak about moral progress unless we make explicit the standard or norm by which we measure it. Contrary to the widespread belief, an a priori value commitment is not an exclusive feature of ethics. It is inherent in any branch of knowledge. The progress in natural sciences is measured by the desirable goal of control of nature for the benefit of man. Behind the study of the structure and interconnection of events is the end in view that such knowledge will alleviate the struggle for survival and implement goods which enhance living. We do not study human history to record for posterity what happened or is happening, but with the goal of discovering specific trends which man may utilize to chart a more rational course of action, by working toward the desirable or counteracting an undesirable trend. We do not study economic depressions, the causes of employment and unemployment with a value-detached attitude, but with the end in view of promoting the desirable ends of an economy, predicated on the valuative commitment that an abundance of goods and a diffused distribution of goods are desirable ends. Psychological, psychiatric, and medical studies are committed to the value that human life is worthy to be preserved, and that certain forms of survival are better. Similarly, ethics is not content to study the various moral practices and beliefs in their historical setting, or in their entanglement of ignorance, superstition, and pragmatic workability. It studies them in the terms of better or worse with the eudaemonistic goal in view that a moral order which increases human happiness is on a higher level than a moral order which brings about a greater misery. It studies the causative agents behind social accord and discord to make valuable contributions toward a better social cohesion, predicated on the fulfillment of the well-being of each single individual. Its ideal directedness is in close contact with realities. Workable solutions for persisting perplexities and ideal projections must come from objective, unbiased studies of social facts. A moral order which could lessen human sufferings and mitigate conflicts is not an order postulated or stipulated at will. It must be discovered in the actualities of social living.

These actualities suggest a continuity of moral values with other values, economic, political, aesthetic, and religious. Moral progress requires an enhancement of all values. The ideals of a greater justice, solidarity, and sociableness find a feeble resonance in people whose basic biological and economic needs are frustrated. Man's progress is "biological, economic and ethical, one and at the same time: an improvement in the societal organization and efficiency and in the equitable social distribution of the advantages of culture, from the collective standpoint, and a qualitative improvement of the individual physically, occupationally and spiritually. The distinction between different levels of progress is a matter of convenience; for both individual and collective experience is single and integral."[1]

There is a coalescence, interpenetration, and interdependence of values. An uplift of morals may lead to a more rational economy, and vice versa, an uplift of economy may lead to deeper social ties. Economic insecurities, unequal distribution of wealth, ostentatious enjoyment of the good things of life by a few and denial of these goods to the vast majority of people—these are the real causes of social conflicts and not an innate pugnacity.

The belief in moral progress in the sense of a uniform transition from savagery to civilization is not true to fact. Within each society we find individuals who hardly surpass the level of a beast. Regressions to more primitive social relations are just as common as progressions to more humane relations. If we concentrate on the first, we may easily despair of a common humanity; if we focus our attention on the latter the hopes for such humanity are kept alive. As a rule the gloomy outlooks prevail over the cheerful ones for many reasons: displaced emotional expectations and disillusionments, international tensions and wars. People are prone to rationalize defeat more readily than success. Disillusionments are thought-arresting stages which paralyze intelligent efforts in coping successfully with perplexities. If we search for the real causes of social discords, their ascertained forces suggest feasible remedies. To know them and not use them is moral transgression. To hypostatize the lack of moral wisdom (in matters pertaining to better social relations) as an immutable human aggressiveness or as the immunity of emotions and attitudes to rational beliefs is to indulge in defeating rationalizations. Moral progress hinges upon the possibility of conquering the moral tribalism, the main agent behind cruelties men mete out to men. Man's bio-psychological oneness calls for an ethical universalism, but the latter is being obstructed for economic, social, and political expediencies. That our moral beliefs very often rationalize our entrenched sentiments and attitudes is very true. But it is also true that our sentiments and attitudes are formed by these beliefs. A modification of moral beliefs in the direction of greater rationality and social efficacy is the most needed change for moral progress. There are many reasons why very often our sentiments and attitudes assert themselves against our better knowledge: emotional fixation, poor self-integration, and an improper sense of reality and values. The most important and most neglected reason is the deplorable fact that the better knowledge remains in the minds of men instead of being embodied in the various social institutions.[2]

NOTES

Chapter I

1. J. Dewey, *Human Nature and Conduct,* New York: The Modern Library, 1950, p. 1.
2. *Ibid.,* p. 95 ff.
3. *Ibid.,* p. 115 ff.
4. "It is in the matter of cooperation that he fails of complete success. Man, like other animals, is filled with impulses and passions which, on the whole, ministered to survival while man was emerging. But his intelligence has shown him that passions are often self-defeating, and that his desires could be more complete if certain of his passions were given less scope and others more. Man has not viewed himself at most times and in most places as a species competing with other species. He has been interested, not in man, but in men; and men have been sharply divided into friends and enemies." (B. Russell, *Human Society in Ethics and Politics,* London: George Allen & Unwin, Ltd., 1954, p. 15.)
5. Clyde Kluckhohn and Others, "Values and Value Orientation in the Theory of Action" (contained in *Toward a General Theory of Action,* edited by Talcott Parsons and Edward A. Shills, Harvard University Press, 1951, p. 418 ff.).
6. Cf. Gardner Murphy, *Human Potentialities,* Basic Books, Inc., 1957, p. 16.
7. *Ibid.,* p. 16.
8. *Ibid.,* p. 18.
9. "Man no doubt is deeply embedded and moulded in the matrix of society. He absorbs, conserves, communicates and bequeathes society. But he also embellishes, enriches, deepens and fabricates it. Society is a changing medium of creation and expression of his deep seated desires, values and aspirations." (Radhakamal Mukerjee, *The Dynamics of Morals,* London: Macmillan & Co., 1950, p. XIX.)
10. Gardner Murphy, "Social Motivation," (contained in *So-*

cial *Psychology*, Cambridge, Mass.: Addison-Wesley Publishing Co., 1954, p. 604).
11. G. Murphy, "Human Potentialities," p. 277.

Chapter II

1. J. Dewey, *Reconstruction in Philosophy*, New York: Mentor Book, 1950, p. 133.
2. Morris Ginsberg, *Reason and Unreason in Society*, London: Longmans, Green & Co., 1947, p. 302 ff.
3. Kurt Baier, *The Moral Point of View*, Ithaca: Cornell University Press, 1958, p. 253.
4. Kurt Baier, *Ibid.*, p. 296.
5. Lewis S. Feuer, *Psychoanalysis and Ethics*, Springfield, Ill.: Charles C. Thomas, 1955, p. 8 ff.

Chapter III

1. Cf. *Feelings and Emotions*, edited by Martin L. Reymert, New York: McGraw-Hill Book Company, 1950, p. 40.
2. Norman Cameron, *The Psychology of Behavior Disorders*, New York: Houghton Mifflin Company, 1947, p. 74.
3. F. J. J. Buytendijk, "The Phenomenological Approach to the Problem of Feelings and Emotions," (contained in *Feelings and Emotions*, edited by Martin L. Reymert, New York: McGraw-Hill Book Company, 1950, p. 129).
4. Trigant Burrow, "Emotion and the Social Crisis: A Problem in Phylobiology, *ibid.*, p. 474.
5. Frederick Paulhan, *The Laws of Feeling*, 1930, p. 157 (translated by C. K. Ogden).

Chapter IV

1. Cf. B. Russell, *Human Society in Ethics and Politics*, p. 27.
2. M. Ginsberg, *Reason and Unreason in Society*, p. 245.
3. Arthur E. Murphy, *The Uses of Reason*, New York: The Macmillan Co., 1943, p. 105.
4. *Ibid.*, p. 135.

Chapter VI

1. S. L. Hart, *Treatise on Values,* New York: Philosophical Library, 1949, p. 44.
2. *Ibid.,* p. 46 ff.
3. Erich Fromm, *The Sane Society,* New York: Rinehart & Co., 1955, p. 201.
4. *Ibid.,* p. 30 ff.
5. B. Russell, *The Conquest of Happiness,* New York: The American Library, 1955, p. 142.

Chapter VII

1. Kurt Baier, "The Moral Point of View," p. 73.
2. William H. Werkmeister, "The Meaning and Being of Values," (published in *Sinn und Sein,* Tübingen: Niemeyer Verlag, 1960, p. 552).
3. S. L. Hart, "Nature and Objectivity of Ethical Judgments," *Philosophy and Phenomenological Research,* Vol. XV, No. 3, p. 363.
4. *Ibid.,* p. 363.
5. *Ibid.,* p. 366.
6. *Ibid.,* p. 366.
7. *Ibid.,* p. 366.
8. S. L. Hart, *Treatise on Values,* p. 19 ff.
9. Cf. Ray Lepley, *Verifiability of Value,* Columbia University, New York, 1944, p. 78 ff.
10. S. L. Hart, *Treatise on Values,* p. 30.
11. *Ibid.,* p. 31
12. J. Dewey, *Reconstruction in Philosophy,* p. 95.
13. J. Dewey, *The Quest for Certainty,* New York: Putnam's Sons, 1929, p. 260 ff.
14. *Ibid.,* p. 262.
15. *Ibid.,* p. 278.

Chapter VIII

1. Cf. Alfred Jules Ayer, *Language, Truth and Logic,* London: Victor Gollancz Ltd., 1950, p. 102 ff.
2. B. Russell, *Human Society in Ethics and Politics,* p. 17 ff.

3. Edwin T. Mitchell, *A System of Ethics,* New York: Charles Scribner's Sons, 1950. p. 88.
4. Cf. E. T. Mitchell, A *System of Ethics,* p. 112 ff.

Chapter IX

1. Edwin T. Mitchell, *A System of Ethics,* p. 8 ff.
2. Bertrand Russell, *Human Society in Ethics and Politics,* p. 17 ff.
3. Melvin Rader, *Ethics and Society,* New York: Henry Holt & Co., 1950, p. 115.
4. S. L. Hart, "Bridging Sociology and Ethics," (published in *The Frontiers of Social Science,* London: Macmillan & Co., 1957, p. 158 ff.
5. Radhakamal Mukerjee, *The Dynamics of Morals,* p. 257 ff.
6. *Ibid.,* p. 3.
7. E. Jordan, *The Good Life,* The Chicago University Press, 1949, p. 13 ff.
8. Cf. Stephen Pepper, *Ethics,* New York: Appleton-Century Crofts, Inc., 1960, p. 26 ff.
9. Bertrand Russell, *Human Society in Ethics and Politics,* p. 128.
10. Lewis Samuel Feuer, *Psychoanalysis and Ethics,* p. 129.

Chapter X

1. Cf. J. Dewey, *Theory of Valuations,* Chicago: Chicago University Press, 1950, p. 43 ff. (contained in *International Encyclopedia of Unified Science,* Vol. II, No. 4).
2. E. Jordan, *The Good Life,* p. 3 ff.
3. Cf. Erich Fromm, *The Sane Society,* p. 14 ff.
4. Cf. W. G. Sumner, *Folkways,* Boston: Ginn and Company, 1906.
5. Stephen Pepper, *Ethics,* p. 68.
6. Cf. A. J. Ayer, *Language, Truth and Logic,* p. 102 ff.

Chapter XI

1. S. L. Hart, *Treatise on Values,* p. 132.

2. S. L. Hart, *Treatise on Values,* p. 134.
3. Cf. Edwin A. Burtt, *Man Seeks the Divine,* New York: Harper and Brothers, 1957, p. 91 ff.
4. Cf. Radhakamal Mukerjee, *The Dynamics of Morals,* London: Macmillan and Co., Ltd., 1950, p. 410 ff.

Chapter XII

1. Radhakamal Mukerjee, *The Social Structure of Values,* London: Macmillan and Co., p. 402.
2. Cf. E. Jordan, *The Good Life,* p. 402 ff.

INDEX

Aristotle, 57, 105
Ayer, A. J., 18f, 15f

Baier, K., 120, 121
Bentham, J., 26
Biological nature, 19
Barrow, T., 120
Kurt, E., 113
Buytendijk, F. J., 120

Character, 85ff
Causality, 55
Culture, 19
Customary morality, 81

Darwin, 22
Determinism, 55
Dewey, J., 5, 119, 120, 121, 122

Emotions, 30ff, 43, 44
Environment, 17ff
Ethical controversies, 80
Ethical hedonism, 45
Ethical rationalism, 45
Ethical references, 9, 10
Ethical relativism, 81ff
Ethical skepticism, 7
Ethical terms, 74ff
Ethical universality, 117
Ethics, S. 7, 84, 105
Ethics, 5, 6, 9, 23, 25, 31, 35, 38, 82, 83, 91, 99

Factual judgments, 25ff
Freud, S., 13, 18

INDEX

Aristotle, 57, 102
Ayer, A. J., 121, 122

Baier K., 120, 121
Bentham J., 26
Biological nature, 19
Burrow, T., 120
Burtt, E., 123
Buytendijk, F. J., 120

Character, 35ff.
Causality, 55
Culture, 19
Customary morality, 81

Darwin, 22
Determinism, 55
Dewey, J., 5, 119, 120, 121, 122

Emotions, 36ff., 43, 44
Environment, 17ff.
Ethical controversies, 30
Ethical hedonism, 45
Ethical rationalism, 45
Ethical reflections, 9, 10
Ethical relativity, 81ff.
Ethical skepticism, 7
Ethical terms, 74ff.
Ethical universality 117
Ethicists, 5, 7, 83, 105
Ethics, 5, 6, 9, 23, 31, 35, 59, 82, 83, 91, 99

Factual judgments, 62ff.
Freud, S., 13, 48

Freedom, 27, 48ff.
Feuer, L., 120
Fromm, E., 122

Ginsberg, M., 120

Habits, 28
Happiness, 34, 42, 57ff.
Hart, S. L., 120, 121, 122, 123
Hartmann, N., 69
Heredity, 17ff.
Historical relativism, 92
Hobbes, Th. 22
Human nature, 14, 15, 20, 22, 23
Human potentialities, 23
Human rights, 34
Hume, D., 105

Ideology, 2, 89ff.
Indeterminism, 55

Jordan, E., 122

Kant, I., 26
Lepley, R., 121
License, 48, 53
Locke, J., 18

Machiavelli, N., 2
Mitchell, E., 122
Moral approvals, 77
Moral choice, 27ff.
Moral conduct, 27ff.
Moral language, 32, 75
Moral optimism, 22
Moral pessimism, 22
Moral progress, 81, 115ff.
Moral thought, 35, 86, 87, 101
Morals, 20, 82, 104
Mukerjee, R., 119, 122, 123
Murphy, G., 119

Murphy, A., 120

Pepper, S., 122
Plato, 5, 31, 69, 89
Pugnacity, 13ff.
Pythagoras, 67

Rader, M., 122
Rationalization, 3
Reason, 3, 45, 46, 47
Rousseau, J., 31
Russell, B., 119, 120, 121, 122
Ryemert, M., 120

Schopenhauer, A., 22
Self-realization, 31, 58
Socrates, 102
Sophists, 102
Social drives, 49
Spinoza, B., 40

Values, 62ff.
Value absolutism, 91
Value judgments, 63, 71, 72, 105, 106
Value objectivity, 91
Value realism, 69
Value subjectivism, 70
Value terms, 65ff.